50 St. Patrick's Day Breakfast Recipes for Home

By: Kelly Johnson

Table of Contents

- Shamrock Pancakes
- Irish Soda Bread French Toast
- Green Smoothie Bowl
- Corned Beef Hash
- Irish Breakfast Burritos
- Spinach and Feta Breakfast Muffins
- Green Eggs and Ham
- Lucky Charms Oatmeal
- Potato and Leek Soup
- Irish Cheddar and Chive Scones
- Green Apple Smoothie
- Corned Beef and Cabbage Hash
- Spinach and Mushroom Quiche
- Shamrock Shakes
- Irish Cream Coffee Cake
- Green Pancake Stack
- Cottage Cheese and Chive Pancakes
- Irish Breakfast Sausages
- Green Tea Smoothie
- Potato Pancakes (Latkes)
- Irish Potato and Ham Soup
- Shamrock Waffles
- Mint Chocolate Chip Muffins
- Avocado Toast with Spinach
- Irish-style Egg and Bacon Sandwiches
- Green Veggie Omelet
- Shamrock Yogurt Parfaits
- Irish Cream and Chocolate Chip Scones
- Spinach and Bacon Breakfast Casserole
- Green Fruit Salad
- Irish Breakfast Porridge
- Creamy Avocado and Spinach Breakfast Wraps
- Shamrock Protein Smoothie
- Irish Breakfast Pizza
- Savory Irish Potato Muffins
- Green Veggie Frittata

- Minty Chocolate Overnight Oats
- Shamrock-shaped Bagels
- Irish Smoked Salmon and Cream Cheese Toast
- Spinach and Cheddar Breakfast Quesadilla
- Green Apple and Cinnamon Breakfast Bars
- Irish Breakfast Tea Cake
- Shamrock and Berry Smoothie
- Potato and Spinach Stuffed Croissants
- Irish Breakfast Baked Oatmeal
- Green Bell Pepper and Onion Frittata
- Minted Yogurt and Berry Parfait
- Irish Ham and Cheese Breakfast Roll-ups
- Green Banana Pancakes
- Shamrock and Herb Scrambled Eggs

Shamrock Pancakes

Ingredients:

- 1 1/2 cups all-purpose flour
- 2 tbsp sugar
- 1 tbsp baking powder
- 1/2 tsp salt
- 1 1/4 cups milk
- 1 egg
- 3 tbsp melted butter
- 1/2 tsp vanilla extract
- Green food coloring
- Butter or oil for cooking

Instructions:

1. **Prepare the Batter:**
    - In a large bowl, whisk together the flour, sugar, baking powder, and salt.
    - In another bowl, combine the milk, egg, melted butter, and vanilla extract.
    - Gradually mix the wet ingredients into the dry ingredients until just combined.
2. **Add Color:**
    - Add a few drops of green food coloring to the batter and stir until the desired shade of green is achieved.
3. **Heat the Pan:**
    - Heat a non-stick skillet or griddle over medium heat and lightly grease it with butter or oil.
4. **Cook the Pancakes:**
    - For shamrock shapes, use a shamrock-shaped cookie cutter or mold to shape the batter on the skillet.
    - Pour a small amount of batter inside the cookie cutter and cook until bubbles form on the surface and the edges look set, about 2-3 minutes.
    - Carefully remove the cookie cutter and flip the pancake. Cook until the other side is golden brown, about 1-2 minutes.
5. **Serve:**
    - Serve warm with your favorite toppings, such as maple syrup, whipped cream, or fresh fruit.

Enjoy your festive and fun Shamrock Pancakes!

Irish Soda Bread French Toast

Ingredients:

- 6 slices Irish soda bread (about 1 inch thick)
- 3 large eggs
- 1 cup milk
- 2 tbsp sugar
- 1 tsp vanilla extract
- 1/2 tsp ground cinnamon
- 1/4 tsp ground nutmeg
- 2 tbsp butter
- Maple syrup, for serving
- Fresh berries, for garnish (optional)
- Powdered sugar, for garnish (optional)

Instructions:

1. **Prepare the Batter:**
   - In a shallow dish, whisk together the eggs, milk, sugar, vanilla extract, cinnamon, and nutmeg.
2. **Soak the Bread:**
   - Dip each slice of Irish soda bread into the egg mixture, ensuring both sides are well-coated. Let it soak briefly to absorb the liquid but not too long to avoid sogginess.
3. **Heat the Pan:**
   - Melt 1 tablespoon of butter in a large skillet or griddle over medium heat.
4. **Cook the French Toast:**
   - Place the soaked bread slices in the skillet and cook until golden brown and crispy on both sides, about 3-4 minutes per side. You may need to add more butter as you cook additional slices.
5. **Serve:**
   - Serve the French toast warm with maple syrup, fresh berries, and a dusting of powdered sugar if desired.

Enjoy your Irish Soda Bread French Toast—a unique twist on a classic breakfast favorite!

Green Smoothie Bowl

Ingredients:

- 1 cup fresh spinach leaves
- 1/2 cup kale leaves (stems removed)
- 1 ripe banana
- 1/2 cup frozen pineapple chunks
- 1/2 cup frozen mango chunks
- 1/2 cup Greek yogurt (plain or vanilla)
- 1/2 cup almond milk (or any milk of your choice)
- 1 tbsp honey or maple syrup (optional, for sweetness)
- 1/2 tsp chia seeds (optional, for added nutrition)

Toppings (optional but recommended):

- Fresh fruit (sliced strawberries, kiwi, blueberries, etc.)
- Granola
- Nuts and seeds (such as almonds, chia seeds, or flaxseeds)
- Shredded coconut
- A drizzle of honey or nut butter

Instructions:

1. **Blend the Smoothie:**
   - In a blender, combine the spinach, kale, banana, frozen pineapple, frozen mango, Greek yogurt, almond milk, and honey (if using).
   - Blend until smooth and creamy. You may need to stop and scrape down the sides or add a bit more milk if the mixture is too thick.
2. **Prepare the Bowl:**
   - Pour the smoothie into a bowl.
3. **Add Toppings:**
   - Arrange your choice of toppings over the surface of the smoothie. Be creative and add a variety of textures and flavors, such as sliced fruit, granola, nuts, seeds, and a sprinkle of shredded coconut.
4. **Serve:**
   - Enjoy immediately with a spoon!

This Green Smoothie Bowl is not only visually appealing but also packed with nutrients, making it a delicious and healthful way to start your day.

Corned Beef Hash

Ingredients:

- 2 cups cooked corned beef, chopped (leftover or pre-cooked)
- 2 cups potatoes, peeled and diced (about 2 medium potatoes)
- 1 small onion, finely chopped
- 1 bell pepper, diced (red or green)
- 2 cloves garlic, minced
- 2 tbsp vegetable oil or butter
- 1 tsp dried thyme
- 1/2 tsp paprika
- Salt and black pepper to taste
- 2 tbsp chopped fresh parsley (optional, for garnish)
- 2-4 large eggs (one per serving, optional)

Instructions:

1. **Cook the Potatoes:**
   - Place the diced potatoes in a pot of salted water. Bring to a boil and cook until tender, about 10 minutes. Drain and set aside.
2. **Prepare the Hash:**
   - Heat the vegetable oil or butter in a large skillet over medium heat.
   - Add the chopped onion, bell pepper, and garlic. Sauté until the onion is translucent and the bell pepper is tender, about 5 minutes.
   - Add the cooked potatoes to the skillet and cook, stirring occasionally, until they begin to brown and crisp up, about 5-7 minutes.
3. **Add the Corned Beef:**
   - Stir in the chopped corned beef, thyme, paprika, salt, and black pepper.
   - Continue to cook, stirring occasionally, until the corned beef is heated through and the mixture is well combined, about 5 minutes.
4. **Optional - Add Eggs:**
   - If you like, you can cook eggs to top the hash. In a separate skillet, cook the eggs to your desired doneness (fried, poached, etc.).
5. **Serve:**
   - Transfer the corned beef hash to plates. Top each serving with a cooked egg if desired.
   - Garnish with chopped fresh parsley, if using.

Enjoy your Corned Beef Hash as a hearty and flavorful breakfast or brunch option!

Irish Breakfast Burritos

Ingredients:

- 4 large flour tortillas
- 4 large eggs
- 4 slices of bacon
- 1 cup cooked breakfast sausages, sliced or crumbled
- 1 cup hash browns or diced potatoes, cooked
- 1 cup black or kidney beans, drained and rinsed (optional)
- 1 cup shredded Irish cheddar cheese (or any sharp cheddar)
- 1/2 cup chopped fresh tomatoes (optional)
- 1/4 cup chopped fresh chives or green onions
- 2 tbsp butter or oil
- Salt and black pepper to taste
- Hot sauce or ketchup (optional, for serving)

Instructions:

1. **Cook the Bacon and Sausage:**
   - In a large skillet over medium heat, cook the bacon until crispy. Remove and drain on paper towels. Once cooled, crumble or chop into pieces.
   - In the same skillet, cook the breakfast sausages until browned and cooked through. Remove and set aside.
2. **Prepare the Hash Browns:**
   - If you're using frozen hash browns, cook according to package instructions. If using fresh potatoes, peel, dice, and cook in a skillet with a little oil until golden and crispy. Set aside.
3. **Scramble the Eggs:**
   - In a bowl, whisk the eggs with a pinch of salt and pepper.
   - Heat butter or oil in a skillet over medium heat. Pour in the eggs and cook, stirring occasionally, until scrambled and just set.
4. **Assemble the Burritos:**
   - Warm the flour tortillas in a dry skillet or microwave.
   - Lay each tortilla flat and layer with a portion of scrambled eggs, bacon, sausage, hash browns, beans (if using), tomatoes (if using), and shredded cheese.
5. **Roll the Burritos:**
   - Fold in the sides of the tortilla, then roll from the bottom up, securing the filling inside.
6. **Heat the Burritos:**
   - In a skillet over medium heat, add a little butter or oil. Place the burritos seam side down and cook until golden brown and crispy, about 2-3 minutes per side.
7. **Serve:**
   - Cut the burritos in half if desired. Serve with hot sauce or ketchup, and garnish with chopped chives or green onions.

Enjoy your Irish Breakfast Burritos for a hearty and satisfying meal with a delicious Irish twist!

Spinach and Feta Breakfast Muffins

Ingredients:

- 1 1/2 cups all-purpose flour
- 1/2 cup whole wheat flour
- 1 tbsp baking powder
- 1/2 tsp salt
- 1/4 tsp black pepper
- 1/2 tsp dried oregano
- 1/2 tsp dried basil
- 1/2 cup milk
- 1/4 cup olive oil
- 2 large eggs
- 1 cup fresh spinach, chopped (or 1/2 cup frozen spinach, thawed and drained)
- 1/2 cup crumbled feta cheese
- 1/4 cup grated Parmesan cheese (optional, for extra flavor)

Instructions:

1. **Preheat Oven:**
   - Preheat your oven to 375°F (190°C). Grease a muffin tin or line it with paper liners.
2. **Prepare the Dry Ingredients:**
   - In a large bowl, whisk together the all-purpose flour, whole wheat flour, baking powder, salt, black pepper, oregano, and basil.
3. **Prepare the Wet Ingredients:**
   - In another bowl, whisk together the milk, olive oil, and eggs until well combined.
4. **Combine Ingredients:**
   - Pour the wet ingredients into the dry ingredients and stir until just combined. The batter will be thick.
   - Gently fold in the chopped spinach and crumbled feta cheese. If using, fold in the grated Parmesan cheese as well.
5. **Fill the Muffin Tin:**
   - Divide the batter evenly among the muffin cups, filling each about 2/3 full.
6. **Bake:**
   - Bake in the preheated oven for 18-22 minutes, or until a toothpick inserted into the center comes out clean and the tops are golden brown.
7. **Cool:**
   - Allow the muffins to cool in the pan for a few minutes before transferring them to a wire rack to cool completely.

These Spinach and Feta Breakfast Muffins are perfect for a quick breakfast or a nutritious snack throughout the day. Enjoy!

Green Eggs and Ham

Ingredients:

- 4 large eggs
- 1/4 cup milk
- 1/2 cup fresh spinach leaves (or kale for a more intense green color)
- 1 tbsp butter or oil
- 4 slices of ham (or substitute with cooked bacon or sausage)
- Salt and black pepper to taste

Instructions:

1. **Prepare the Spinach:**
    - In a blender or food processor, combine the fresh spinach and milk. Blend until smooth and the mixture is green. This will be used to color the eggs.
2. **Prepare the Eggs:**
    - In a bowl, whisk together the eggs, spinach mixture, salt, and black pepper until well combined.
3. **Cook the Ham:**
    - In a large skillet over medium heat, cook the slices of ham until they are heated through and slightly crispy, about 1-2 minutes per side. Remove and set aside.
4. **Cook the Green Eggs:**
    - In the same skillet, add the butter or oil and heat over medium-low heat.
    - Pour the green egg mixture into the skillet. Cook, stirring gently, until the eggs are scrambled and just set. Avoid overcooking to keep the eggs fluffy.
5. **Serve:**
    - Serve the green eggs with the slices of ham on the side. You can also serve with toast or fresh fruit for a complete breakfast.

Enjoy this playful and colorful breakfast that's sure to bring a smile to your face!

Lucky Charms Oatmeal

Ingredients:

- 1 cup old-fashioned oats
- 2 cups milk (or any milk of your choice)
- 1/2 cup water
- 1/4 cup brown sugar or honey (adjust to taste)
- 1/2 tsp vanilla extract
- A pinch of salt
- 1 cup Lucky Charms cereal
- Fresh fruit or additional toppings (optional)

Instructions:

1. **Cook the Oats:**
   - In a medium saucepan, combine the oats, milk, water, brown sugar or honey, vanilla extract, and a pinch of salt.
   - Bring to a boil over medium heat, then reduce the heat and simmer, stirring occasionally, until the oats are tender and have absorbed the liquid, about 5-7 minutes.
2. **Add the Cereal:**
   - Stir in the Lucky Charms cereal. Cook for an additional 1-2 minutes until the cereal is slightly softened but still has some crunch.
3. **Serve:**
   - Spoon the oatmeal into bowls. Top with extra Lucky Charms cereal for added crunch, and add fresh fruit or other toppings if desired.
4. **Optional – Garnish:**
   - Garnish with a drizzle of honey or a sprinkle of cinnamon for extra flavor.

Enjoy this whimsical and colorful oatmeal that's perfect for celebrating St. Patrick's Day or just adding a bit of fun to your breakfast routine!

Potato and Leek Soup

Ingredients:

- 2 tbsp olive oil or unsalted butter
- 3 leeks, white and light green parts only, cleaned and sliced
- 3 cloves garlic, minced
- 4 cups peeled and diced potatoes (about 4 medium potatoes)
- 4 cups vegetable or chicken broth
- 1 cup milk or cream (adjust for desired creaminess)
- Salt and black pepper to taste
- 1/4 cup chopped fresh parsley or chives (optional, for garnish)
- Croutons or sliced baguette (optional, for serving)

Instructions:

1. **Prepare the Leeks:**
    - Clean the leeks thoroughly to remove any dirt. Slice them thinly and set aside.
2. **Cook the Aromatics:**
    - In a large pot, heat the olive oil or butter over medium heat.
    - Add the sliced leeks and cook, stirring occasionally, until they are soft and translucent, about 5-7 minutes.
    - Add the minced garlic and cook for another minute until fragrant.
3. **Add the Potatoes and Broth:**
    - Add the diced potatoes to the pot and stir to combine with the leeks.
    - Pour in the vegetable or chicken broth and bring to a boil. Reduce the heat and simmer until the potatoes are tender, about 15-20 minutes.
4. **Blend the Soup:**
    - Use an immersion blender to puree the soup directly in the pot until smooth. Alternatively, you can transfer the soup in batches to a blender. Be cautious with hot liquids and blend in batches if using a traditional blender.
5. **Add Creaminess:**
    - Stir in the milk or cream to achieve the desired creaminess. Adjust the seasoning with salt and black pepper to taste. Heat the soup through.
6. **Serve:**
    - Ladle the soup into bowls and garnish with chopped fresh parsley or chives if desired.
    - Serve with croutons or a slice of baguette for added texture.

Enjoy your homemade Potato and Leek Soup, a perfect blend of creamy, savory flavors!

Irish Cheddar and Chive Scones

Ingredients:

- 2 1/2 cups all-purpose flour
- 1/4 cup granulated sugar
- 1 tbsp baking powder
- 1/2 tsp salt
- 1/2 tsp black pepper
- 1/2 cup (1 stick) cold unsalted butter, cubed
- 1 cup shredded Irish cheddar cheese (or sharp cheddar)
- 1/4 cup chopped fresh chives
- 3/4 cup milk (or buttermilk for a richer flavor)
- 1 large egg
- 1 tbsp milk (for brushing, optional)
- Extra shredded cheese for topping (optional)

Instructions:

1. **Preheat Oven:**
   - Preheat your oven to 400°F (200°C). Line a baking sheet with parchment paper or lightly grease it.
2. **Prepare Dry Ingredients:**
   - In a large bowl, whisk together the flour, sugar, baking powder, salt, and black pepper.
3. **Cut in the Butter:**
   - Add the cold, cubed butter to the dry ingredients. Use a pastry cutter, two forks, or your fingers to cut the butter into the flour mixture until it resembles coarse crumbs.
4. **Add Cheese and Chives:**
   - Stir in the shredded cheddar cheese and chopped chives until evenly distributed.
5. **Mix Wet Ingredients:**
   - In a separate bowl, whisk together the milk and egg. Pour this mixture into the dry ingredients.
6. **Form the Dough:**
   - Gently mix until just combined. Be careful not to overwork the dough; it should be slightly sticky but manageable.
7. **Shape and Cut:**
   - Turn the dough onto a lightly floured surface and pat it into a circle about 1-inch thick. Use a floured knife or pizza cutter to cut the dough into wedges or squares.
8. **Transfer and Bake:**
   - Transfer the scones to the prepared baking sheet. Brush the tops with a bit of milk and sprinkle with extra shredded cheese if desired.
9. **Bake:**

- Bake in the preheated oven for 15-20 minutes, or until the scones are golden brown and cooked through.
10. **Cool:**
    - Allow the scones to cool slightly on a wire rack before serving.

These Irish Cheddar and Chive Scones are delightful when served warm with a bit of butter or on their own. Enjoy them for a savory breakfast or as a tasty accompaniment to soups and salads!

Green Apple Smoothie

Ingredients:

- 2 1/2 cups all-purpose flour
- 1/4 cup granulated sugar
- 1 tbsp baking powder
- 1/2 tsp salt
- 1/2 tsp black pepper
- 1/2 cup (1 stick) cold unsalted butter, cubed
- 1 cup shredded Irish cheddar cheese (or sharp cheddar)
- 1/4 cup chopped fresh chives
- 3/4 cup milk (or buttermilk for a richer flavor)
- 1 large egg
- 1 tbsp milk (for brushing, optional)
- Extra shredded cheese for topping (optional)

Instructions:

1. **Preheat Oven:**
    - Preheat your oven to 400°F (200°C). Line a baking sheet with parchment paper or lightly grease it.
2. **Prepare Dry Ingredients:**
    - In a large bowl, whisk together the flour, sugar, baking powder, salt, and black pepper.
3. **Cut in the Butter:**
    - Add the cold, cubed butter to the dry ingredients. Use a pastry cutter, two forks, or your fingers to cut the butter into the flour mixture until it resembles coarse crumbs.
4. **Add Cheese and Chives:**
    - Stir in the shredded cheddar cheese and chopped chives until evenly distributed.
5. **Mix Wet Ingredients:**
    - In a separate bowl, whisk together the milk and egg. Pour this mixture into the dry ingredients.
6. **Form the Dough:**
    - Gently mix until just combined. Be careful not to overwork the dough; it should be slightly sticky but manageable.
7. **Shape and Cut:**
    - Turn the dough onto a lightly floured surface and pat it into a circle about 1-inch thick. Use a floured knife or pizza cutter to cut the dough into wedges or squares.
8. **Transfer and Bake:**
    - Transfer the scones to the prepared baking sheet. Brush the tops with a bit of milk and sprinkle with extra shredded cheese if desired.
9. **Bake:**

- Bake in the preheated oven for 15-20 minutes, or until the scones are golden brown and cooked through.
10. **Cool:**
    - Allow the scones to cool slightly on a wire rack before serving.

These Irish Cheddar and Chive Scones are delightful when served warm with a bit of butter or on their own. Enjoy them for a savory breakfast or as a tasty accompaniment to soups and salads!

Green Apple Smoothie

Ingredients:

- 1 large green apple, cored and chopped (leave the skin on for extra fiber)
- 1 cup fresh spinach or kale leaves (for added greens)
- 1/2 cucumber, peeled and chopped
- 1/2 banana (for natural sweetness and creaminess)
- 1/2 cup Greek yogurt (plain or vanilla)
- 1/2 cup almond milk (or any milk of your choice)
- 1 tbsp honey or maple syrup (optional, for added sweetness)
- Juice of 1/2 lemon (to add a fresh, tangy flavor)
- Ice cubes (optional, for a chilled smoothie)

Instructions:

1. **Prepare the Ingredients:**
   - Wash and chop the green apple, cucumber, and banana. If using spinach or kale, wash the leaves thoroughly.
2. **Blend:**
   - In a blender, combine the green apple, spinach or kale, cucumber, banana, Greek yogurt, almond milk, honey or maple syrup (if using), and lemon juice.
   - Blend until smooth and creamy. If you prefer a thinner consistency, you can add a little more milk.
3. **Adjust Consistency and Sweetness:**
   - Taste the smoothie and adjust the sweetness by adding more honey or maple syrup if needed.
   - For a colder smoothie, add a few ice cubes and blend again until the ice is crushed and the smoothie is chilled.
4. **Serve:**
   - Pour the smoothie into glasses and serve immediately.

Enjoy your Green Apple Smoothie as a refreshing and nutritious start to your day or a healthy pick-me-up anytime!

Corned Beef and Cabbage Hash

Ingredients:

- 2 cups cooked corned beef, chopped (leftover or pre-cooked)
- 2 cups cooked potatoes, diced (about 2 medium potatoes)
- 2 cups cooked cabbage, chopped (leftover or pre-cooked)
- 1 medium onion, diced
- 1 bell pepper, diced (red or green)
- 2 cloves garlic, minced
- 2 tbsp vegetable oil or unsalted butter
- 1 tsp dried thyme
- 1/2 tsp paprika
- Salt and black pepper to taste
- 2 tbsp chopped fresh parsley (optional, for garnish)
- 2-4 large eggs (one per serving, optional)

Instructions:

1. **Prepare the Ingredients:**
   - Dice the cooked corned beef and cooked potatoes. Chop the cooked cabbage. If not using leftovers, cook and prepare these ingredients as needed.
2. **Cook the Vegetables:**
   - In a large skillet, heat the vegetable oil or butter over medium heat.
   - Add the diced onion and bell pepper. Cook, stirring occasionally, until the onion is translucent and the bell pepper is tender, about 5 minutes.
   - Add the minced garlic and cook for another minute until fragrant.
3. **Add the Potatoes and Cabbage:**
   - Stir in the diced potatoes and chopped cabbage. Cook, stirring occasionally, until the potatoes start to brown and crisp up, about 5-7 minutes.
4. **Add the Corned Beef:**
   - Add the chopped corned beef, dried thyme, paprika, salt, and black pepper. Stir to combine all the ingredients. Cook for an additional 5-7 minutes, allowing the flavors to meld and the corned beef to heat through.
5. **Optional – Cook the Eggs:**
   - If you like, you can cook eggs to top the hash. In a separate skillet, cook the eggs to your desired doneness (fried, poached, or scrambled).
6. **Serve:**
   - Serve the corned beef and cabbage hash hot, topped with a cooked egg if desired.
   - Garnish with chopped fresh parsley if using.

Enjoy this hearty and flavorful Corned Beef and Cabbage Hash as a satisfying breakfast, brunch, or even dinner!

Spinach and Mushroom Quiche

Ingredients:

For the Crust:

- 1 1/2 cups all-purpose flour
- 1/2 tsp salt
- 1/2 cup (1 stick) cold unsalted butter, cubed
- 1/4 cup cold water (more if needed)

For the Filling:

- 1 tbsp olive oil
- 1 cup mushrooms, sliced
- 2 cups fresh spinach, chopped
- 1 small onion, finely chopped
- 2 cloves garlic, minced
- 1 cup shredded cheese (cheddar, Swiss, or your choice)
- 4 large eggs
- 1 cup heavy cream (or half-and-half)
- Salt and black pepper to taste
- 1/4 tsp dried thyme or basil (optional)

Instructions:

1. **Prepare the Crust:**
    - Preheat your oven to 375°F (190°C).
    - In a medium bowl, whisk together the flour and salt.
    - Cut in the cold butter using a pastry cutter or your fingers until the mixture resembles coarse crumbs.
    - Gradually add cold water, 1 tablespoon at a time, until the dough just comes together.
    - Form the dough into a disk, wrap in plastic wrap, and refrigerate for at least 30 minutes.
2. **Prebake the Crust:**
    - On a lightly floured surface, roll out the dough to fit a 9-inch pie dish or tart pan.
    - Transfer the dough to the pan, pressing it into the edges. Trim any excess dough.
    - Prick the bottom of the crust with a fork to prevent bubbling.
    - Bake the crust in the preheated oven for 10-12 minutes until lightly golden. Remove from the oven and set aside.
3. **Prepare the Filling:**
    - While the crust is baking, heat olive oil in a large skillet over medium heat.
    - Add the onions and cook until translucent, about 3-4 minutes.

- Add the mushrooms and cook until they release their moisture and start to brown, about 5 minutes.
    - Add the garlic and cook for another minute until fragrant.
    - Stir in the chopped spinach and cook until wilted. Remove from heat and let cool slightly.
4. **Assemble the Quiche:**
    - In a large bowl, whisk together the eggs, heavy cream, salt, black pepper, and dried thyme or basil (if using).
    - Stir in the cooked spinach and mushroom mixture and shredded cheese.
    - Pour the filling into the pre-baked crust, spreading it evenly.
5. **Bake:**
    - Return the quiche to the oven and bake for 30-35 minutes, or until the filling is set and the top is golden brown.
    - Let the quiche cool for a few minutes before slicing.
6. **Serve:**
    - Serve warm or at room temperature. Enjoy with a side salad or fresh fruit for a complete meal.

This Spinach and Mushroom Quiche is flavorful, versatile, and perfect for any occasion.

Shamrock Shakes

Ingredients:

- 2 cups vanilla ice cream
- 1 cup milk (whole milk or your preferred type)
- 1/2 tsp peppermint extract (adjust to taste)
- Green food coloring (a few drops for color)
- Whipped cream (optional, for topping)
- Maraschino cherries (optional, for garnish)

Instructions:

1. **Blend the Shake:**
    - In a blender, combine the vanilla ice cream, milk, and peppermint extract.
    - Blend until smooth and creamy.
2. **Add Color:**
    - Add a few drops of green food coloring to the blender. Blend again until the color is evenly distributed. Adjust the number of drops to achieve your desired shade of green.
3. **Serve:**
    - Pour the Shamrock Shake into glasses.
    - Top with whipped cream if desired and garnish with a maraschino cherry.
4. **Enjoy:**
    - Serve immediately with a straw.

This simple and delightful Shamrock Shake is perfect for celebrating St. Patrick's Day or just enjoying a fun, minty treat!

Irish Cream Coffee Cake

Ingredients:

For the Cake:

- 2 1/2 cups all-purpose flour
- 1 cup granulated sugar
- 1/2 cup unsalted butter, softened
- 1 cup sour cream
- 2 large eggs
- 1/2 cup Irish cream liqueur (such as Baileys)
- 1/2 tsp baking powder
- 1 tsp baking soda
- 1/2 tsp salt
- 1 tsp vanilla extract

For the Streusel Topping:

- 1/2 cup brown sugar
- 1/2 cup all-purpose flour
- 1/4 cup unsalted butter, cold and cubed
- 1/2 tsp ground cinnamon
- 1/4 cup chopped pecans or walnuts (optional)

For the Glaze (optional):

- 1/2 cup powdered sugar
- 2-3 tbsp Irish cream liqueur
- 1/2 tsp vanilla extract

Instructions:

1. **Preheat Oven:**
   - Preheat your oven to 350°F (175°C). Grease and flour a 9-inch round cake pan or a 9x13-inch baking dish.
2. **Prepare the Streusel Topping:**
   - In a medium bowl, combine the brown sugar, flour, and ground cinnamon.
   - Cut in the cold, cubed butter using a pastry cutter or your fingers until the mixture resembles coarse crumbs.
   - Stir in the chopped nuts if using. Set aside.
3. **Make the Cake Batter:**
   - In a large bowl, cream together the softened butter and granulated sugar until light and fluffy.
   - Add the eggs one at a time, beating well after each addition.
   - Mix in the vanilla extract and Irish cream liqueur.

- In a separate bowl, whisk together the flour, baking powder, baking soda, and salt.
- Gradually add the dry ingredients to the wet ingredients, alternating with the sour cream, beginning and ending with the dry ingredients. Mix until just combined.

4. **Assemble the Cake:**
    - Pour half of the batter into the prepared pan and smooth it out.
    - Sprinkle half of the streusel topping over the batter.
    - Add the remaining batter and smooth the top.
    - Sprinkle the remaining streusel topping evenly over the top.
5. **Bake:**
    - Bake in the preheated oven for 35-45 minutes, or until a toothpick inserted into the center of the cake comes out clean and the top is golden brown.
6. **Prepare the Glaze (optional):**
    - While the cake is baking, mix the powdered sugar, Irish cream liqueur, and vanilla extract in a small bowl until smooth.
    - Adjust the consistency with more liqueur or powdered sugar if needed.
7. **Cool and Glaze:**
    - Allow the cake to cool in the pan for about 10 minutes before transferring it to a wire rack to cool completely.
    - Once cooled, drizzle with the Irish cream glaze if desired.

Enjoy your Irish Cream Coffee Cake with a cup of coffee or tea for a delightful treat!

Green Pancake Stack

Ingredients:

For the Pancakes:

- 1 1/2 cups all-purpose flour
- 2 tbsp granulated sugar
- 1 tbsp baking powder
- 1/2 tsp salt
- 1 cup milk (whole milk or any milk of your choice)
- 1 large egg
- 2 tbsp melted butter or vegetable oil
- 1/2 cup fresh spinach leaves, packed (for natural green color) or a few drops of green food coloring (if using)
- 1 tsp vanilla extract

For Serving:

- Maple syrup or honey
- Fresh fruit (such as strawberries, blueberries, or bananas)
- Whipped cream (optional)
- Extra green food coloring or powdered sugar for garnish (optional)

Instructions:

1. **Prepare the Spinach (if using):**
   - If using spinach for natural color, blend the spinach leaves with a small amount of milk until smooth. You should get about 1/2 cup of spinach puree.
2. **Make the Pancake Batter:**
   - In a large bowl, whisk together the flour, sugar, baking powder, and salt.
   - In another bowl, combine the milk, egg, melted butter, and vanilla extract.
   - If using spinach puree, add it to the wet ingredients. If using food coloring, add a few drops to the wet ingredients.
   - Pour the wet ingredients into the dry ingredients and stir until just combined. The batter may be slightly lumpy, which is okay.
3. **Cook the Pancakes:**
   - Heat a non-stick skillet or griddle over medium heat and lightly grease with butter or oil.
   - Pour 1/4 cup of batter onto the skillet for each pancake. Cook until bubbles form on the surface and the edges look set, about 2-3 minutes.
   - Flip the pancakes and cook for an additional 1-2 minutes, or until golden brown and cooked through.
   - Repeat with the remaining batter, greasing the skillet as needed.
4. **Serve:**

- Stack the pancakes on a plate. Serve with maple syrup or honey, fresh fruit, and whipped cream if desired.
- For extra festive touches, garnish with a sprinkle of powdered sugar or a few extra drops of green food coloring on top.

Enjoy your fun and colorful Green Pancake Stack!

Cottage Cheese and Chive Pancakes

Ingredients:

- 1 cup all-purpose flour
- 1 tbsp baking powder
- 1/2 tsp salt
- 1/4 tsp black pepper
- 1 cup cottage cheese (small curd)
- 1/2 cup milk (or buttermilk for extra tanginess)
- 2 large eggs
- 2 tbsp chopped fresh chives (or more to taste)
- 2 tbsp melted butter or vegetable oil (plus more for cooking)

Instructions:

1. **Prepare the Dry Ingredients:**
   - In a large bowl, whisk together the flour, baking powder, salt, and black pepper.
2. **Mix the Wet Ingredients:**
   - In another bowl, combine the cottage cheese, milk, and eggs. Stir until well mixed.
3. **Combine the Ingredients:**
   - Pour the wet ingredients into the dry ingredients. Stir until just combined. Be careful not to overmix; the batter should be slightly lumpy.
   - Fold in the chopped chives and melted butter or oil.
4. **Cook the Pancakes:**
   - Heat a non-stick skillet or griddle over medium heat. Lightly grease with butter or oil.
   - Pour 1/4 cup of batter onto the skillet for each pancake. Spread the batter slightly if needed.
   - Cook until bubbles form on the surface and the edges look set, about 2-3 minutes.
   - Flip the pancakes and cook for an additional 1-2 minutes, or until golden brown and cooked through.
   - Repeat with the remaining batter, greasing the skillet as needed.
5. **Serve:**
   - Serve the pancakes warm with your favorite toppings. They pair well with sour cream, extra chives, or even a light salad for a complete meal.

These Cottage Cheese and Chive Pancakes offer a delicious and savory alternative to traditional sweet pancakes, and they're perfect for a satisfying breakfast or brunch. Enjoy!

Irish Breakfast Sausages

Ingredients:

- 1 lb (450 g) ground pork (preferably with a bit of fat for juiciness)
- 1/2 lb (225 g) ground veal (or you can use more pork)
- 1 small onion, finely chopped
- 1/4 cup fresh breadcrumbs (or oatmeal for a more traditional texture)
- 2 cloves garlic, minced
- 1 tsp dried sage
- 1 tsp dried thyme
- 1/2 tsp ground white pepper
- 1/2 tsp ground black pepper
- 1/4 tsp ground nutmeg
- 1/4 tsp ground allspice
- 1/4 cup fresh parsley, finely chopped (optional)
- 1/2 cup cold water or beef broth
- Sausage casings (optional, for stuffing, or you can shape into patties if preferred)

Instructions:

1. **Prepare the Sausage Mixture:**
   - In a large bowl, combine the ground pork and veal.
   - Add the finely chopped onion, breadcrumbs (or oatmeal), and minced garlic.
   - Stir in the sage, thyme, white pepper, black pepper, nutmeg, allspice, and parsley if using.
   - Gradually add the cold water or beef broth to the mixture, stirring until the mixture is well combined and has a slightly sticky texture.
2. **Stuff the Sausage Casings (if using):**
   - If using sausage casings, rinse and soak them according to the package instructions. Then, slide the casings onto a sausage stuffer attachment.
   - Stuff the sausage casings with the sausage mixture, being careful not to overstuff. Twist the sausages into links of your desired length.
   - Tie the ends of the casings with kitchen twine.
3. **Shape into Patties (if not using casings):**
   - If not using casings, shape the sausage mixture into patties of your preferred size.
4. **Cook the Sausages:**
   - Heat a skillet over medium heat and add a little oil if necessary.
   - Cook the sausages in batches (whether links or patties) for 10-12 minutes, turning occasionally, until they are browned and cooked through to an internal temperature of 160°F (71°C).
5. **Serve:**

- Serve the Irish breakfast sausages with traditional accompaniments such as eggs, black and white pudding, baked beans, tomatoes, and toast for a hearty Irish breakfast.

Enjoy your homemade Irish Breakfast Sausages as part of a classic breakfast spread or on their own as a delicious treat!

Green Tea Smoothie

Ingredients:

- 1 cup brewed green tea, cooled (or matcha green tea powder for a more intense flavor)
- 1 banana, peeled and sliced
- 1/2 cup fresh spinach or kale leaves
- 1/2 cup frozen pineapple chunks (or mango for a different flavor)
- 1/2 cup Greek yogurt (plain or vanilla)
- 1 tbsp honey or maple syrup (optional, for sweetness)
- 1/2 tsp chia seeds or flaxseeds (optional, for added nutrition)
- Ice cubes (optional, for a colder smoothie)

Instructions:

1. **Prepare the Green Tea:**
   - Brew a cup of green tea according to the package instructions. Let it cool to room temperature or chill it in the refrigerator.
2. **Blend the Ingredients:**
   - In a blender, combine the cooled green tea, banana, spinach or kale, frozen pineapple, and Greek yogurt.
   - If you prefer a sweeter smoothie, add honey or maple syrup.
   - Add chia seeds or flaxseeds if using.
3. **Blend Until Smooth:**
   - Blend on high until all ingredients are well combined and the smoothie is smooth and creamy. If you want a colder, thicker smoothie, add a few ice cubes and blend again.
4. **Serve:**
   - Pour the smoothie into glasses and serve immediately.
5. **Garnish (optional):**
   - Garnish with a slice of pineapple or a sprinkle of chia seeds on top for extra flair.

This Green Tea Smoothie is not only delicious but also packed with antioxidants and nutrients, making it a great choice for a healthful and satisfying drink. Enjoy!

Potato Pancakes (Latkes)

Ingredients:

- 4 large russet potatoes
- 1 small onion
- 2 large eggs
- 1/4 cup all-purpose flour
- 1/4 cup matzo meal (or more flour if preferred)
- 1 tsp salt
- 1/2 tsp black pepper
- 1/2 tsp baking powder (optional, for extra crispiness)
- Vegetable oil (for frying)

Instructions:

1. **Prepare the Potatoes and Onion:**
   - Peel the potatoes and grate them using a box grater or food processor.
   - Place the grated potatoes in a large bowl of cold water to prevent browning.
   - Grate the onion and add it to the bowl with the potatoes.
2. **Drain and Squeeze:**
   - After grating, drain the potatoes and onion using a fine-mesh strainer or cheesecloth.
   - Squeeze out as much excess moisture as possible. The drier the mixture, the crispier the latkes will be.
3. **Mix the Ingredients:**
   - In a large bowl, combine the grated potatoes and onion with eggs, flour, matzo meal, salt, black pepper, and baking powder if using.
   - Stir until everything is well combined.
4. **Heat the Oil:**
   - Heat about 1/4 inch of vegetable oil in a large skillet or frying pan over medium-high heat. You want the oil to be hot but not smoking.
5. **Form and Fry the Latkes:**
   - Scoop a small amount of the potato mixture (about 1/4 cup) and form it into a patty, pressing it down slightly.
   - Carefully place the patties into the hot oil, being sure not to overcrowd the pan. Fry in batches if necessary.
   - Cook the latkes for about 3-4 minutes per side, or until they are golden brown and crispy.
6. **Drain and Serve:**
   - Remove the latkes from the skillet and place them on a plate lined with paper towels to drain excess oil.
   - Serve hot with traditional accompaniments such as applesauce, sour cream, or a sprinkle of fresh herbs.

Enjoy your homemade Potato Pancakes (Latkes) as a delicious and crispy treat!

Irish Potato and Ham Soup

Ingredients:

- 2 tbsp unsalted butter
- 1 medium onion, diced
- 2 cloves garlic, minced
- 3 cups potatoes, peeled and diced (about 4 medium potatoes)
- 1 large carrot, diced
- 1 celery stalk, diced
- 4 cups chicken or vegetable broth
- 1 cup cooked ham, diced (use leftover ham or pre-cooked ham)
- 1 cup whole milk or heavy cream (for a richer soup)
- 1/2 tsp dried thyme
- 1/2 tsp dried rosemary
- 1 bay leaf
- Salt and black pepper to taste
- 2 tbsp chopped fresh parsley (optional, for garnish)

Instructions:

1. **Prepare the Vegetables:**
   - Peel and dice the potatoes, and dice the carrot and celery.
2. **Cook the Aromatics:**
   - In a large pot or Dutch oven, melt the butter over medium heat.
   - Add the diced onion and cook until translucent, about 5 minutes.
   - Stir in the minced garlic and cook for an additional 1 minute until fragrant.
3. **Add Vegetables and Broth:**
   - Add the diced potatoes, carrot, and celery to the pot.
   - Pour in the chicken or vegetable broth.
   - Add the dried thyme, rosemary, and bay leaf.
   - Bring the mixture to a boil, then reduce the heat to a simmer.
4. **Simmer:**
   - Simmer the soup for about 15-20 minutes, or until the potatoes and vegetables are tender.
5. **Add Ham and Cream:**
   - Stir in the diced ham and continue to cook for another 5 minutes to heat the ham through.
   - Remove the bay leaf.
   - Stir in the milk or heavy cream, and adjust the seasoning with salt and black pepper to taste. Heat the soup until warmed through but do not boil after adding the cream.
6. **Serve:**
   - Ladle the soup into bowls and garnish with chopped fresh parsley if desired.
   - Serve hot with crusty bread or crackers on the side.

This Irish Potato and Ham Soup is a satisfying and flavorful dish that's perfect for warming up on a chilly day. Enjoy!

Shamrock Waffles

Ingredients:

- 2 cups all-purpose flour
- 2 tbsp granulated sugar
- 1 tbsp baking powder
- 1/2 tsp salt
- 2 large eggs
- 1 3/4 cups milk (whole milk or any milk of your choice)
- 1/2 cup unsalted butter, melted
- 1 tsp vanilla extract
- 1/2 tsp peppermint extract (optional, for a hint of mint flavor)
- Green food coloring (a few drops, or to your desired color)

Instructions:

1. **Preheat the Waffle Iron:**
   - Preheat your waffle iron according to the manufacturer's instructions.
2. **Prepare the Dry Ingredients:**
   - In a large bowl, whisk together the flour, sugar, baking powder, and salt.
3. **Prepare the Wet Ingredients:**
   - In another bowl, beat the eggs and then add the milk, melted butter, vanilla extract, and peppermint extract (if using).
   - Stir in a few drops of green food coloring until you reach your desired shade of green.
4. **Combine Ingredients:**
   - Pour the wet ingredients into the dry ingredients and mix until just combined. The batter may be slightly lumpy, which is okay. Do not overmix.
5. **Cook the Waffles:**
   - Lightly grease the waffle iron with non-stick spray or brush it with a little oil.
   - Pour the batter onto the preheated waffle iron according to the manufacturer's directions. Typically, about 1/2 cup to 1 cup of batter per waffle works well.
   - Close the waffle iron and cook until the waffles are golden brown and crispy. Cooking times will vary depending on your waffle iron.
6. **Serve:**
   - Serve the Shamrock Waffles warm with your favorite toppings. Suggestions include fresh fruit, whipped cream, syrup, or a dusting of powdered sugar.
7. **Garnish (optional):**
   - For extra festive flair, you can top the waffles with a dollop of whipped cream and a sprinkle of green sugar or edible glitter.

Enjoy your Shamrock Waffles as a delightful and festive breakfast or brunch treat!

Mint Chocolate Chip Muffins

Ingredients:

- 2 cups all-purpose flour
- 2 tbsp granulated sugar
- 1 tbsp baking powder
- 1/2 tsp salt
- 2 large eggs
- 1 3/4 cups milk (whole milk or any milk of your choice)
- 1/2 cup unsalted butter, melted
- 1 tsp vanilla extract
- 1/2 tsp peppermint extract (optional, for a hint of mint flavor)
- Green food coloring (a few drops, or to your desired color)

Instructions:

1. **Preheat the Waffle Iron:**
   - Preheat your waffle iron according to the manufacturer's instructions.
2. **Prepare the Dry Ingredients:**
   - In a large bowl, whisk together the flour, sugar, baking powder, and salt.
3. **Prepare the Wet Ingredients:**
   - In another bowl, beat the eggs and then add the milk, melted butter, vanilla extract, and peppermint extract (if using).
   - Stir in a few drops of green food coloring until you reach your desired shade of green.
4. **Combine Ingredients:**
   - Pour the wet ingredients into the dry ingredients and mix until just combined. The batter may be slightly lumpy, which is okay. Do not overmix.
5. **Cook the Waffles:**
   - Lightly grease the waffle iron with non-stick spray or brush it with a little oil.
   - Pour the batter onto the preheated waffle iron according to the manufacturer's directions. Typically, about 1/2 cup to 1 cup of batter per waffle works well.
   - Close the waffle iron and cook until the waffles are golden brown and crispy. Cooking times will vary depending on your waffle iron.
6. **Serve:**
   - Serve the Shamrock Waffles warm with your favorite toppings. Suggestions include fresh fruit, whipped cream, syrup, or a dusting of powdered sugar.
7. **Garnish (optional):**
   - For extra festive flair, you can top the waffles with a dollop of whipped cream and a sprinkle of green sugar or edible glitter.

Enjoy your Shamrock Waffles as a delightful and festive breakfast or brunch treat!

Mint Chocolate Chip Muffins

Ingredients:

- 1 3/4 cups all-purpose flour
- 1/2 cup granulated sugar
- 1/4 cup brown sugar
- 2 tsp baking powder
- 1/2 tsp baking soda
- 1/2 tsp salt
- 1/2 cup unsalted butter, melted and slightly cooled
- 2 large eggs
- 1 cup buttermilk (or milk with 1 tbsp lemon juice or vinegar)
- 1/2 tsp mint extract (adjust to taste)
- 1/2 tsp vanilla extract
- 1/2 cup mini chocolate chips
- Optional: green food coloring (a few drops for a festive look)

Instructions:

1. **Preheat Oven:**
    - Preheat your oven to 375°F (190°C).
    - Line a 12-cup muffin tin with paper liners or lightly grease it.
2. **Prepare Dry Ingredients:**
    - In a large bowl, whisk together the flour, granulated sugar, brown sugar, baking powder, baking soda, and salt.
3. **Prepare Wet Ingredients:**
    - In another bowl, whisk together the melted butter, eggs, buttermilk, mint extract, and vanilla extract. If using green food coloring, add a few drops here.
4. **Combine Ingredients:**
    - Pour the wet ingredients into the dry ingredients and stir until just combined. The batter will be lumpy, and that's okay.
    - Gently fold in the mini chocolate chips.
5. **Fill Muffin Cups:**
    - Divide the batter evenly among the muffin cups, filling each about 2/3 full.
6. **Bake:**
    - Bake in the preheated oven for 18-20 minutes, or until a toothpick inserted into the center of a muffin comes out clean and the tops are golden brown.
7. **Cool and Serve:**
    - Allow the muffins to cool in the pan for 5 minutes before transferring them to a wire rack to cool completely.
    - Serve warm or at room temperature.

These Mint Chocolate Chip Muffins are a delightful blend of minty freshness and rich chocolate, perfect for adding a special touch to your breakfast or snack time. Enjoy!

Avocado Toast with Spinach

Ingredients:

- 2 ripe avocados
- 1 tbsp lemon juice (or lime juice)
- Salt and black pepper to taste
- 1/4 tsp garlic powder (optional)
- 1/4 tsp crushed red pepper flakes (optional, for a bit of heat)
- 2 cups fresh spinach leaves
- 4 slices of whole grain or your favorite bread (sourdough, multigrain, etc.)
- 1 tbsp olive oil (for sautéing spinach)
- 1-2 cloves garlic, minced (optional, for extra flavor)
- Optional toppings: cherry tomatoes, radishes, poached egg, feta cheese, or fresh herbs

Instructions:

1. **Prepare the Avocado Mixture:**
    - Cut the avocados in half, remove the pit, and scoop the flesh into a bowl.
    - Mash the avocado with a fork until it reaches your desired level of smoothness.
    - Stir in the lemon juice, salt, black pepper, garlic powder, and crushed red pepper flakes (if using). Mix well.
2. **Cook the Spinach:**
    - Heat the olive oil in a skillet over medium heat.
    - Add the minced garlic (if using) and cook for about 30 seconds until fragrant.
    - Add the fresh spinach leaves and sauté until wilted, about 2-3 minutes. Season with a pinch of salt and pepper.
3. **Toast the Bread:**
    - Toast the slices of bread until golden brown and crispy. You can use a toaster, toaster oven, or grill the bread in a skillet.
4. **Assemble the Toast:**
    - Spread a generous layer of the mashed avocado mixture on each slice of toasted bread.
    - Top with a portion of sautéed spinach.
5. **Add Optional Toppings:**
    - If desired, add additional toppings such as sliced cherry tomatoes, radishes, a poached egg, crumbled feta cheese, or fresh herbs.
6. **Serve:**
    - Serve the avocado toast immediately while the bread is still crispy.

Enjoy your Avocado Toast with Spinach as a tasty and nutritious meal that's both satisfying and packed with flavor!

Irish-style Egg and Bacon Sandwiches

Ingredients:

- 4 slices of Irish bacon (or substitute with Canadian bacon or regular bacon)
- 4 large eggs
- 4 slices of soda bread or crusty bread (like sourdough or whole grain)
- 2 tbsp unsalted butter (for frying and spreading)
- Salt and black pepper to taste
- Optional toppings: grilled tomatoes, black pudding (blood sausage), sautéed mushrooms

Instructions:

1. **Cook the Bacon:**
   - Heat a skillet over medium heat.
   - Add the bacon slices and cook until crispy and browned, about 3-4 minutes per side.
   - Remove the bacon from the skillet and set aside on a paper towel-lined plate to drain.
2. **Cook the Eggs:**
   - In the same skillet with some of the bacon fat (or use a bit of butter if needed), crack the eggs into the skillet.
   - Cook the eggs to your desired doneness. For sunny-side-up eggs, cook until the whites are set but the yolks are still runny. For over-easy or over-hard eggs, flip the eggs gently and cook for an additional 1-2 minutes.
3. **Prepare the Bread:**
   - While the eggs are cooking, spread butter on the slices of bread.
   - Toast the bread in a separate skillet or toaster until golden brown and crispy.
4. **Assemble the Sandwiches:**
   - Place a slice of toasted bread on each plate.
   - Top each slice with a few slices of crispy bacon.
   - Carefully place a cooked egg on top of the bacon.
   - Season with a little salt and black pepper.
5. **Add Optional Toppings (if using):**
   - If desired, add grilled tomatoes, sautéed mushrooms, or slices of black pudding to the sandwiches for extra flavor.
6. **Finish and Serve:**
   - Top with another slice of toasted bread if you prefer a sandwich, or serve open-faced.
   - Serve warm.

These Irish-style Egg and Bacon Sandwiches are perfect for a hearty breakfast or brunch, offering a satisfying combination of flavors and textures. Enjoy!

Green Veggie Omelet

Ingredients:

- 3 large eggs
- 1/4 cup milk or water
- Salt and black pepper to taste
- 1 tbsp olive oil or butter (for cooking)
- 1/2 cup fresh spinach, chopped
- 1/4 cup broccoli florets, finely chopped
- 1/4 cup green bell pepper, diced
- 1/4 cup zucchini, diced
- 2 tbsp green onions, chopped
- 1/4 cup shredded cheese (optional, such as cheddar or feta)
- 1 clove garlic, minced (optional)

Instructions:

1. **Prepare the Eggs:**
   - In a bowl, whisk together the eggs, milk (or water), salt, and black pepper until well combined.
2. **Cook the Vegetables:**
   - Heat the olive oil or butter in a non-stick skillet over medium heat.
   - Add the garlic (if using) and cook for about 30 seconds until fragrant.
   - Add the broccoli, green bell pepper, zucchini, and green onions. Sauté for 3-4 minutes until the vegetables are tender and slightly browned.
   - Stir in the chopped spinach and cook for an additional 1-2 minutes until the spinach is wilted.
3. **Make the Omelet:**
   - Push the vegetables to one side of the skillet, or remove them if you prefer.
   - Pour the egg mixture into the skillet, tilting the pan to spread the eggs evenly.
   - Cook without stirring until the edges start to set, about 2 minutes. You can lift the edges of the omelet gently with a spatula to let any uncooked egg flow to the edges.
   - Once the bottom is set but the top is still slightly runny, sprinkle the cheese (if using) over one half of the omelet.
4. **Fold and Serve:**
   - Gently fold the omelet in half over the filling.
   - Cook for an additional 1-2 minutes until the cheese is melted and the omelet is cooked through.
   - Slide the omelet onto a plate and serve immediately.

Optional Toppings:

- Garnish with fresh herbs like chives, parsley, or cilantro.

- Serve with a side of avocado slices or a light salad for extra freshness.

This Green Veggie Omelet is both flavorful and packed with nutrients, making it a great choice for a healthy and satisfying meal. Enjoy!

Shamrock Yogurt Parfaits

Ingredients:

- 3 large eggs
- 1/4 cup milk or water
- Salt and black pepper to taste
- 1 tbsp olive oil or butter (for cooking)
- 1/2 cup fresh spinach, chopped
- 1/4 cup broccoli florets, finely chopped
- 1/4 cup green bell pepper, diced
- 1/4 cup zucchini, diced
- 2 tbsp green onions, chopped
- 1/4 cup shredded cheese (optional, such as cheddar or feta)
- 1 clove garlic, minced (optional)

Instructions:

1. **Prepare the Eggs:**
    - In a bowl, whisk together the eggs, milk (or water), salt, and black pepper until well combined.
2. **Cook the Vegetables:**
    - Heat the olive oil or butter in a non-stick skillet over medium heat.
    - Add the garlic (if using) and cook for about 30 seconds until fragrant.
    - Add the broccoli, green bell pepper, zucchini, and green onions. Sauté for 3-4 minutes until the vegetables are tender and slightly browned.
    - Stir in the chopped spinach and cook for an additional 1-2 minutes until the spinach is wilted.
3. **Make the Omelet:**
    - Push the vegetables to one side of the skillet, or remove them if you prefer.
    - Pour the egg mixture into the skillet, tilting the pan to spread the eggs evenly.
    - Cook without stirring until the edges start to set, about 2 minutes. You can lift the edges of the omelet gently with a spatula to let any uncooked egg flow to the edges.
    - Once the bottom is set but the top is still slightly runny, sprinkle the cheese (if using) over one half of the omelet.
4. **Fold and Serve:**
    - Gently fold the omelet in half over the filling.
    - Cook for an additional 1-2 minutes until the cheese is melted and the omelet is cooked through.
    - Slide the omelet onto a plate and serve immediately.

Optional Toppings:

- Garnish with fresh herbs like chives, parsley, or cilantro.

- Serve with a side of avocado slices or a light salad for extra freshness.

This Green Veggie Omelet is both flavorful and packed with nutrients, making it a great choice for a healthy and satisfying meal. Enjoy!

Shamrock Yogurt Parfaits

Ingredients:

- 2 cups Greek yogurt (plain or vanilla)
- 1-2 tbsp honey or maple syrup (optional, for sweetness)
- 1/2 tsp vanilla extract
- 1/2 cup fresh spinach leaves (for natural green color)
- 1 cup granola
- 1 cup fresh fruit (such as berries, kiwi, or sliced bananas)
- Optional: green food coloring (if desired for a more vibrant green)

Instructions:

1. **Prepare the Green Yogurt:**
    - In a blender or food processor, combine the Greek yogurt, honey (if using), vanilla extract, and fresh spinach leaves.
    - Blend until smooth. The spinach will give the yogurt a natural green color.
    - If you prefer a more intense green color, you can add a few drops of green food coloring and blend again.
2. **Assemble the Parfaits:**
    - In serving glasses or bowls, start by spooning a layer of the green yogurt mixture.
    - Add a layer of granola over the yogurt.
    - Top with a layer of fresh fruit.
3. **Repeat Layers:**
    - Repeat the layers with the remaining yogurt, granola, and fruit until the glasses or bowls are filled.
4. **Garnish and Serve:**
    - Garnish with a few extra pieces of fruit on top, and a sprinkle of granola for added crunch.
    - Serve immediately or refrigerate for up to a few hours before serving.

Optional Additions:

- Add a drizzle of honey or a sprinkle of chia seeds on top for extra flavor and texture.
- Use fresh mint leaves as a garnish for a refreshing touch.

These Shamrock Yogurt Parfaits are not only delicious and nutritious but also visually appealing, making them perfect for a St. Patrick's Day celebration or any time you want a fun and healthy treat!

Irish Cream and Chocolate Chip Scones

Ingredients:

- 2 1/2 cups all-purpose flour
- 1/3 cup granulated sugar
- 1 tbsp baking powder
- 1/2 tsp salt
- 1/2 cup unsalted butter, cold and cut into small cubes
- 1/2 cup mini chocolate chips
- 1/2 cup Irish cream liqueur (such as Baileys) or Irish cream-flavored coffee creamer
- 1 large egg
- 1 tsp vanilla extract
- 1/4 cup whole milk (or as needed)
- Optional: extra granulated sugar for sprinkling on top

Instructions:

1. **Preheat Oven:**
    - Preheat your oven to 400°F (200°C).
    - Line a baking sheet with parchment paper or lightly grease it.
2. **Prepare the Dry Ingredients:**
    - In a large bowl, whisk together the flour, granulated sugar, baking powder, and salt.
3. **Cut in the Butter:**
    - Add the cold butter cubes to the dry ingredients.
    - Using a pastry cutter or your fingertips, cut the butter into the flour mixture until it resembles coarse crumbs with pea-sized pieces of butter.
4. **Add Chocolate Chips:**
    - Gently fold in the mini chocolate chips.
5. **Prepare the Wet Ingredients:**
    - In a separate bowl, whisk together the Irish cream liqueur (or coffee creamer), egg, and vanilla extract.
6. **Combine Wet and Dry Ingredients:**
    - Pour the wet ingredients into the dry ingredients and stir until just combined. The dough should be somewhat shaggy.
    - If the dough is too dry, add whole milk a tablespoon at a time until it comes together. Be careful not to overmix.
7. **Shape and Cut the Scones:**
    - Turn the dough out onto a lightly floured surface and gently knead it a few times to bring it together.
    - Pat the dough into a 1-inch thick circle or rectangle.
    - Cut the dough into 8-12 wedges or use a round cutter to cut out individual scones.
8. **Bake the Scones:**

- Place the scones onto the prepared baking sheet, spacing them a few inches apart.
- If desired, sprinkle a little granulated sugar on top of each scone for a sweet crunch.
- Bake in the preheated oven for 15-20 minutes, or until the scones are golden brown and a toothpick inserted into the center comes out clean.

9. **Cool and Serve:**
    - Allow the scones to cool slightly on a wire rack before serving.

These Irish Cream and Chocolate Chip Scones offer a delightful combination of rich Irish cream flavor and sweet chocolate chips, making them a perfect treat for any occasion. Enjoy!

Spinach and Bacon Breakfast Casserole

Ingredients:

- 6 slices of bacon
- 1 small onion, diced
- 2 cups fresh spinach, chopped
- 6 large eggs
- 1 cup milk (whole milk or any milk of your choice)
- 1 cup shredded cheddar cheese (or cheese of your choice)
- 1/2 tsp garlic powder
- 1/2 tsp dried thyme or oregano
- Salt and black pepper to taste
- 4 cups cubed bread (such as day-old baguette, sourdough, or whole wheat)
- Optional: 1/4 cup grated Parmesan cheese for topping

Instructions:

1. **Preheat Oven:**
    - Preheat your oven to 350°F (175°C).
    - Grease a 9x13-inch baking dish or casserole dish.
2. **Cook the Bacon:**
    - In a large skillet, cook the bacon over medium heat until crispy. Remove the bacon from the skillet and place it on a paper towel-lined plate to drain.
    - Once cooled, crumble the bacon into bite-sized pieces.
3. **Cook the Vegetables:**
    - In the same skillet, remove excess bacon fat, leaving about 1 tablespoon in the skillet.
    - Add the diced onion and cook until softened, about 3-4 minutes.
    - Add the chopped spinach and cook until wilted, about 2 minutes. Remove from heat.
4. **Prepare the Egg Mixture:**
    - In a large bowl, whisk together the eggs and milk until well combined.
    - Stir in the shredded cheese, garlic powder, dried thyme (or oregano), salt, and black pepper.
5. **Assemble the Casserole:**
    - Spread the cubed bread evenly in the greased baking dish.
    - Evenly distribute the cooked onion and spinach mixture over the bread cubes.
    - Sprinkle the crumbled bacon on top.
    - Pour the egg mixture evenly over the bread, spinach, and bacon.
6. **Add Optional Topping:**
    - If using, sprinkle the grated Parmesan cheese over the top of the casserole for extra flavor and a golden crust.
7. **Bake:**

- Bake in the preheated oven for 30-40 minutes, or until the casserole is set in the center and the top is golden brown.
8. **Cool and Serve:**
    - Allow the casserole to cool for a few minutes before serving. This will help it set and make it easier to cut into squares.

This Spinach and Bacon Breakfast Casserole is both flavorful and satisfying, making it a great choice for feeding a crowd or enjoying as a meal prep option. Enjoy!

Green Fruit Salad

Ingredients:

- 1 green apple, cored and diced
- 1 cup green grapes, halved if large
- 1 kiwi, peeled and sliced
- 1 cup honeydew melon, diced
- 1/2 cup cucumber, peeled and diced (optional for a crunchy texture)
- 1/4 cup fresh mint leaves, chopped (optional for added freshness)
- Juice of 1 lime (for a tangy flavor and to prevent browning)
- 1 tbsp honey or agave syrup (optional, for added sweetness)
- Optional: 1/4 cup pistachios or walnuts, chopped (for added crunch)

Instructions:

1. **Prepare the Fruits:**
   - Dice the green apple, peel and slice the kiwi, and dice the honeydew melon.
   - If using cucumber, peel and dice it as well.
   - Halve the green grapes if they are large.
2. **Mix the Fruit:**
   - In a large mixing bowl, combine all the prepared fruits: green apple, green grapes, kiwi, honeydew melon, and cucumber (if using).
3. **Add Mint and Lime Juice:**
   - If desired, add the chopped fresh mint leaves for a burst of flavor.
   - Drizzle the lime juice over the fruit mixture. This not only adds flavor but also helps to prevent the apple from browning.
4. **Sweeten (Optional):**
   - If you prefer a sweeter salad, drizzle honey or agave syrup over the fruit and gently toss to combine.
5. **Add Nuts (Optional):**
   - For added texture, sprinkle chopped pistachios or walnuts on top before serving.
6. **Serve:**
   - Gently toss the fruit salad to mix the ingredients.
   - Serve immediately for the freshest taste, or chill in the refrigerator for up to 1 hour before serving.

This Green Fruit Salad is a refreshing and nutritious option that showcases a variety of green fruits. It's perfect for a light snack or as a complement to other dishes at brunch or a festive gathering. Enjoy!

Irish Breakfast Porridge

Ingredients:

- 1 cup steel-cut oats
- 2 1/2 cups water
- 1/2 cup milk (whole milk or any milk of your choice)
- 1/4 tsp salt
- 1-2 tbsp brown sugar or honey (optional, for sweetness)
- 1/2 tsp ground cinnamon (optional)
- Fresh fruit, nuts, or seeds for topping (e.g., berries, bananas, almonds)
- Optional: a splash of cream or additional milk for serving

Instructions:

1. **Prepare the Oats:**
   - In a medium saucepan, bring the water to a boil.
2. **Cook the Oats:**
   - Stir in the steel-cut oats and salt.
   - Reduce the heat to low and simmer uncovered for about 20-30 minutes, stirring occasionally, until the oats are tender and have absorbed most of the liquid. Steel-cut oats have a chewy texture and take longer to cook than rolled oats.
3. **Add Milk and Sweetener:**
   - Stir in the milk and cook for an additional 5 minutes, allowing the porridge to become creamy. Adjust the consistency with more milk if necessary.
   - Add brown sugar or honey to taste, and ground cinnamon if desired. Mix well.
4. **Serve:**
   - Spoon the porridge into bowls and add your favorite toppings. Fresh fruit, nuts, seeds, and a drizzle of honey or maple syrup are great options.
5. **Optional Finish:**
   - For extra creaminess, you can add a splash of cream or additional milk before serving.

Topping Ideas:

- Fresh berries (strawberries, blueberries, raspberries)
- Sliced bananas
- Chopped nuts (almonds, walnuts, pecans)
- Seeds (chia seeds, flaxseeds)
- Dried fruits (raisins, apricots)
- A dollop of yogurt

Irish Breakfast Porridge is a hearty and nutritious way to start your day, providing a good source of fiber and energy. Enjoy it warm with your favorite toppings for a satisfying breakfast!

Creamy Avocado and Spinach Breakfast Wraps

Ingredients:

- 2 large tortillas or wraps (whole wheat, spinach, or your choice)
- 1 ripe avocado
- 1 cup fresh spinach leaves
- 2 large eggs (optional, for added protein)
- 1/4 cup shredded cheese (optional, such as cheddar or feta)
- 1 tbsp olive oil or butter (for cooking eggs, if using)
- Salt and black pepper to taste
- 1/2 tsp garlic powder or onion powder (optional, for extra flavor)
- Optional toppings: sliced tomatoes, red onion, hot sauce, or fresh herbs (like cilantro or chives)

Instructions:

1. **Prepare the Avocado:**
    - Cut the avocado in half, remove the pit, and scoop the flesh into a bowl.
    - Mash the avocado with a fork until smooth. Season with a pinch of salt and black pepper to taste.
2. **Cook the Eggs (if using):**
    - Heat the olive oil or butter in a skillet over medium heat.
    - Crack the eggs into the skillet and cook until the whites are set and the yolks are cooked to your liking. You can scramble or cook the eggs sunny-side-up based on your preference.
    - Season the eggs with a pinch of salt, black pepper, and garlic powder or onion powder if desired.
3. **Assemble the Wraps:**
    - Warm the tortillas in a dry skillet or microwave for a few seconds to make them more pliable.
    - Spread a generous layer of mashed avocado on each tortilla.
    - Add a handful of fresh spinach leaves on top of the avocado.
    - If using, place the cooked eggs on top of the spinach. Sprinkle with shredded cheese if desired.
    - Add any additional toppings like sliced tomatoes, red onion, or fresh herbs.
4. **Wrap and Serve:**
    - Fold in the sides of the tortilla and then roll it up from the bottom to enclose the filling.
    - Cut the wraps in half diagonally and serve immediately.

Optional Variations:

- **Add Protein:** Include cooked bacon, ham, or turkey for extra protein.
- **Add Veggies:** Sautéed mushrooms, bell peppers, or onions make great additions.

- **Spicy Kick:** Add hot sauce or a sprinkle of red pepper flakes for a bit of heat.

These Creamy Avocado and Spinach Breakfast Wraps are versatile, nutritious, and easy to make, perfect for a satisfying start to your day! Enjoy!

Shamrock Protein Smoothie

Ingredients:

- 1 cup fresh spinach (or kale for a different green flavor)
- 1 ripe banana
- 1/2 cup Greek yogurt (plain or vanilla)
- 1 scoop protein powder (vanilla or unflavored)
- 1/2 cup frozen pineapple chunks
- 1/2 cup frozen mango chunks
- 1 cup almond milk (or any milk of your choice)
- 1 tbsp chia seeds or flaxseeds (optional, for added fiber and omega-3s)
- 1-2 tbsp honey or maple syrup (optional, for added sweetness)
- Ice cubes (optional, for a thicker consistency)

Instructions:

1. **Prepare Ingredients:**
     - Peel the banana and break it into chunks.
     - Measure out the spinach, yogurt, and protein powder.
2. **Blend:**
     - In a blender, combine the spinach, banana, Greek yogurt, protein powder, frozen pineapple chunks, and frozen mango chunks.
     - Add the almond milk and blend until smooth. If you prefer a thicker smoothie, you can add a few ice cubes and blend again.
3. **Sweeten (Optional):**
     - Taste the smoothie and add honey or maple syrup if you want additional sweetness. Blend again to mix.
4. **Add Seeds (Optional):**
     - Add chia seeds or flaxseeds for extra nutrition and blend briefly to incorporate.
5. **Serve:**
     - Pour the smoothie into a glass and serve immediately.

Optional Garnishes:

- Fresh mint leaves or a slice of lime on the rim of the glass.
- A sprinkle of granola or a few extra chia seeds on top.

This Shamrock Protein Smoothie is not only visually appealing with its green color but also packed with nutrients and protein, making it a perfect choice for a healthy and satisfying drink. Enjoy!

Irish Breakfast Pizza

Ingredients:

- 1 pizza dough (store-bought or homemade)
- 1 tbsp olive oil
- 1/2 cup tomato sauce or pizza sauce
- 1 cup shredded cheddar cheese (or Irish cheddar if available)
- 4 slices of bacon
- 2-3 large eggs
- 1/2 cup black pudding or blood sausage, sliced (optional)
- 1/2 cup cooked sausage or breakfast links, sliced (optional)
- 1/2 cup diced potatoes, pre-cooked (optional)
- 1/4 cup chopped fresh parsley or chives (for garnish)
- Salt and black pepper to taste

Instructions:

1. **Preheat Oven:**
    - Preheat your oven to 475°F (245°C). If using a pizza stone, place it in the oven while it heats.
2. **Cook the Bacon:**
    - In a skillet over medium heat, cook the bacon until crispy. Remove from the skillet and place on a paper towel-lined plate to drain. Once cooled, crumble or chop into pieces.
3. **Prepare the Dough:**
    - Roll out the pizza dough on a floured surface to your desired thickness and shape. If using a pizza stone, transfer the dough to a piece of parchment paper for easy handling.
4. **Assemble the Pizza:**
    - Brush the pizza dough with olive oil.
    - Spread a thin layer of tomato sauce over the dough, leaving a border around the edges.
    - Sprinkle the shredded cheddar cheese evenly over the sauce.
5. **Add Toppings:**
    - Distribute the cooked bacon, sliced black pudding (if using), sausage slices, and diced potatoes (if using) evenly over the cheese.
6. **Bake the Pizza:**
    - Transfer the pizza to the preheated oven or onto the pizza stone if using.
    - Bake for 12-15 minutes, or until the crust is golden and crispy and the cheese is melted and bubbly.
7. **Add the Eggs:**
    - If you want to add eggs, crack them gently onto the pizza about 5 minutes before the pizza is done baking. You can either make small wells in the toppings for the

eggs or carefully place them on top. Continue baking until the eggs are cooked to your liking (sunny-side-up or slightly set).
8. **Garnish and Serve:**
    - Remove the pizza from the oven and let it cool slightly.
    - Garnish with fresh parsley or chives, and season with a little salt and black pepper if desired.
    - Slice and serve warm.

Optional Additions:

- **Vegetables:** Add sautéed mushrooms, bell peppers, or onions for extra flavor.
- **Cheese Varieties:** Experiment with different cheeses such as mozzarella or gouda.

This Irish Breakfast Pizza is a fun and flavorful twist on traditional breakfast fare, combining beloved Irish ingredients with the classic appeal of pizza. Enjoy!

Savory Irish Potato Muffins

Ingredients:

- 1 large russet potato, peeled and diced
- 1 cup all-purpose flour
- 1/2 cup whole wheat flour
- 1/2 cup shredded cheddar cheese (Irish cheddar if available)
- 1/4 cup chopped fresh chives or green onions
- 1/2 tsp baking powder
- 1/2 tsp baking soda
- 1/2 tsp salt
- 1/4 tsp black pepper
- 1/4 tsp garlic powder (optional)
- 1/4 cup melted butter or olive oil
- 1/2 cup milk
- 1 large egg

Instructions:

1. **Preheat Oven:**
   - Preheat your oven to 375°F (190°C).
   - Grease a 12-cup muffin tin or line it with paper liners.
2. **Prepare the Potato:**
   - Boil the diced potato in salted water until tender, about 10 minutes.
   - Drain the potato and mash it until smooth. Allow it to cool slightly.
3. **Mix Dry Ingredients:**
   - In a large bowl, whisk together the all-purpose flour, whole wheat flour, baking powder, baking soda, salt, black pepper, and garlic powder (if using).
4. **Mix Wet Ingredients:**
   - In a separate bowl, whisk together the melted butter or olive oil, milk, and egg.
5. **Combine Ingredients:**
   - Add the mashed potato, shredded cheese, and chopped chives to the wet ingredients and mix well.
   - Fold the wet ingredients into the dry ingredients until just combined. Do not overmix.
6. **Fill Muffin Tin:**
   - Spoon the batter into the prepared muffin tin, filling each cup about 2/3 full.
7. **Bake:**
   - Bake in the preheated oven for 18-22 minutes, or until a toothpick inserted into the center of a muffin comes out clean and the tops are golden brown.
8. **Cool and Serve:**
   - Allow the muffins to cool in the tin for 5 minutes before transferring them to a wire rack to cool completely.

These Savory Irish Potato Muffins are fluffy on the inside with a savory cheese and potato flavor that makes them a standout addition to any meal. They're perfect for a hearty breakfast or as an accompaniment to soups and stews. Enjoy!

Green Veggie Frittata

Ingredients:

- 1 tbsp olive oil
- 1 small onion, diced
- 2 cloves garlic, minced
- 1 cup fresh spinach, chopped
- 1 cup broccoli florets, chopped
- 1/2 cup green bell pepper, diced
- 1/2 cup zucchini, diced
- 6 large eggs
- 1/4 cup milk (whole milk or any milk of your choice)
- 1/2 cup shredded cheese (such as feta, cheddar, or mozzarella)
- 1/4 cup fresh parsley or chives, chopped (optional, for garnish)
- Salt and black pepper to taste
- Optional: 1/4 tsp red pepper flakes for a bit of heat

Instructions:

1. **Preheat Oven:**
   - Preheat your oven to 375°F (190°C).
2. **Cook the Vegetables:**
   - Heat the olive oil in an oven-safe skillet over medium heat.
   - Add the diced onion and cook until softened, about 3-4 minutes.
   - Add the minced garlic and cook for an additional 1 minute until fragrant.
   - Add the chopped spinach, broccoli florets, green bell pepper, and zucchini. Cook until the vegetables are tender, about 5-7 minutes. Season with salt and black pepper to taste.
3. **Prepare the Egg Mixture:**
   - In a large bowl, whisk together the eggs and milk until well combined.
   - Stir in the shredded cheese and season with additional salt and black pepper. If using, add red pepper flakes for a bit of heat.
4. **Combine and Cook:**
   - Pour the egg mixture over the cooked vegetables in the skillet. Stir gently to combine and ensure the eggs are evenly distributed.
5. **Bake:**
   - Transfer the skillet to the preheated oven and bake for 15-20 minutes, or until the frittata is set in the center and the top is golden brown.
6. **Cool and Serve:**
   - Remove the frittata from the oven and let it cool slightly before slicing.
   - Garnish with fresh parsley or chives if desired.
7. **Optional:**
   - Serve with a side of mixed greens or a light salad for a complete meal.

This Green Veggie Frittata is versatile, so feel free to swap in your favorite green vegetables or add other ingredients like cooked bacon, ham, or tomatoes. It's a great way to enjoy a healthy and flavorful meal with minimal effort!

Minty Chocolate Overnight Oats

Ingredients:

- 1/2 cup rolled oats
- 1/2 cup milk (or any plant-based milk like almond, soy, or oat)
- 1/2 cup plain Greek yogurt (or any yogurt of your choice)
- 1 tbsp cocoa powder
- 1-2 tbsp maple syrup or honey (adjust to taste)
- 1/4 tsp peppermint extract (adjust to taste)
- 2 tbsp mini chocolate chips or chopped dark chocolate
- Optional toppings: fresh mint leaves, additional chocolate chips, or sliced bananas

Instructions:

1. **Mix Ingredients:**
    - In a medium bowl or a mason jar, combine the rolled oats, milk, Greek yogurt, cocoa powder, and maple syrup or honey. Stir well until all ingredients are fully mixed and the cocoa powder is dissolved.
2. **Add Mint Flavor:**
    - Stir in the peppermint extract. Start with 1/4 teaspoon and adjust to taste if you prefer a stronger mint flavor.
3. **Add Chocolate:**
    - Mix in the mini chocolate chips or chopped dark chocolate.
4. **Refrigerate:**
    - Cover the bowl or jar with a lid and refrigerate overnight, or for at least 4 hours, to allow the oats to soak and soften.
5. **Serve:**
    - In the morning, give the oats a good stir. If the mixture is too thick, you can add a splash of milk to reach your desired consistency.
6. **Add Toppings:**
    - Top with fresh mint leaves, additional chocolate chips, or sliced bananas if desired.

Tips:

- **Adjust Sweetness:** You can adjust the sweetness by adding more or less maple syrup or honey, according to your taste.
- **Mint Freshness:** If you prefer fresh mint flavor, you can also stir in a few finely chopped fresh mint leaves right before serving.
- **Chocolate Varieties:** Experiment with different types of chocolate or add a spoonful of chocolate spread for extra indulgence.

Minty Chocolate Overnight Oats are a fun and flavorful way to start your day with a nutritious breakfast that feels like a treat. Enjoy!

Shamrock-shaped Bagels

Ingredients:

- 1 1/2 cups warm water (110°F or 45°C)
- 2 tbsp granulated sugar
- 2 tsp active dry yeast
- 3 1/2 cups all-purpose flour (plus extra for dusting)
- 1 tsp salt
- 2 tbsp olive oil
- Green food coloring (optional, for festive color)
- 1 egg, beaten (for egg wash)
- Sesame seeds or poppy seeds (optional, for sprinkling)

Instructions:

1. **Prepare Yeast Mixture:**
    - In a small bowl, combine the warm water and granulated sugar. Sprinkle the yeast over the top and let it sit for 5-10 minutes, until it becomes frothy.
2. **Mix Dough:**
    - In a large bowl, combine the flour and salt.
    - Make a well in the center and pour in the yeast mixture and olive oil. If using green food coloring, add a few drops to the liquid mixture before combining.
    - Mix until a dough forms.
3. **Knead Dough:**
    - Turn the dough out onto a lightly floured surface and knead for about 5-7 minutes, until it is smooth and elastic.
4. **First Rise:**
    - Place the dough in a lightly oiled bowl, cover with a clean kitchen towel, and let it rise in a warm place for about 1 hour, or until doubled in size.
5. **Shape Bagels:**
    - Preheat your oven to 425°F (220°C) and line a baking sheet with parchment paper.
    - Punch down the risen dough and divide it into 8 equal pieces.
    - Roll each piece into a ball and then flatten it slightly. Use a floured rolling pin to roll each piece into a shamrock shape (or use a shamrock-shaped cookie cutter for a more precise shape).
    - Use a small round cutter or a bottle cap to cut out the center of each shamrock to form the bagel hole.
6. **Boil Bagels:**
    - Bring a large pot of water to a boil. Add a tablespoon of sugar to the water if desired.
    - Carefully drop a few bagels into the boiling water at a time and boil for about 1-2 minutes on each side. Use a slotted spoon to remove them and place them on the prepared baking sheet.

7. **Apply Egg Wash:**
    - Brush each bagel with the beaten egg and sprinkle with sesame seeds or poppy seeds if desired.
8. **Bake:**
    - Bake in the preheated oven for 15-20 minutes, or until the bagels are golden brown and cooked through.
9. **Cool:**
    - Let the bagels cool on a wire rack before serving.

Tips:

- **Green Color:** If you want the bagels to be green, add a few drops of green food coloring to the yeast mixture or the dough. Adjust the color to your liking.
- **Shape Variations:** If you don't have a shamrock-shaped cutter, you can shape the dough into traditional round bagels or use other fun shapes if desired.

These Shamrock-Shaped Bagels are a festive and delicious way to celebrate St. Patrick's Day or add a bit of fun to your baking routine. Enjoy them fresh from the oven with your favorite spreads!

Irish Smoked Salmon and Cream Cheese Toast

Ingredients:

- 4 slices of your favorite bread (sourdough, rye, or whole grain work well)
- 4 oz (115g) cream cheese, softened
- 4 oz (115g) Irish smoked salmon, sliced
- 1 small red onion, thinly sliced
- Capers (optional)
- Fresh dill or chives, chopped (for garnish)
- Lemon wedges (for serving)
- Salt and black pepper to taste

Instructions:

1. **Toast the Bread:**
    - Toast the slices of bread until they are golden brown and crispy. You can use a toaster, oven, or even a grill for this.
2. **Prepare the Cream Cheese:**
    - Spread a generous layer of softened cream cheese evenly over each slice of toasted bread.
3. **Add Smoked Salmon:**
    - Arrange slices of Irish smoked salmon on top of the cream cheese.
4. **Add Toppings:**
    - Scatter thin slices of red onion over the salmon.
    - Add capers if desired for a tangy touch.
    - Season with a little salt and freshly ground black pepper.
5. **Garnish:**
    - Sprinkle with fresh dill or chives for a burst of flavor and color.
6. **Serve:**
    - Serve the toast with lemon wedges on the side for squeezing over the top. The lemon adds a bright, fresh flavor that complements the richness of the salmon.

Tips:

- **Choosing Bread:** Opt for a hearty bread that can hold up to the toppings. Sourdough and rye are great choices, but you can use any bread you prefer.
- **Cream Cheese Variations:** You can mix in some herbs or spices into the cream cheese for added flavor. Chopped fresh dill, chives, or even a bit of garlic powder can enhance the taste.
- **Additional Toppings:** Try adding thin slices of cucumber or a few cherry tomatoes for extra freshness and color.

This Irish Smoked Salmon and Cream Cheese Toast is a simple yet elegant dish that pairs wonderfully with a light salad or a cup of tea. Enjoy this delightful treat!

Spinach and Cheddar Breakfast Quesadilla

Ingredients:

- 2 large flour tortillas
- 1 cup shredded cheddar cheese (or any cheese of your choice)
- 1 cup fresh spinach leaves, chopped
- 2 large eggs
- 1/4 cup milk (or any milk of your choice)
- 1 tbsp olive oil or butter
- Salt and black pepper to taste
- Optional: 1/4 cup diced onions, bell peppers, or mushrooms
- Optional: Salsa or sour cream for serving

Instructions:

1. **Prepare the Eggs:**
    - In a bowl, whisk together the eggs, milk, salt, and black pepper until well combined.
2. **Cook the Spinach:**
    - Heat a non-stick skillet over medium heat. Add a small amount of olive oil or butter.
    - If using additional vegetables (onions, bell peppers, mushrooms), sauté them until they are soft and slightly caramelized, about 3-5 minutes.
    - Add the chopped spinach to the skillet and cook until wilted, about 1-2 minutes. Remove the vegetables and spinach from the skillet and set aside.
3. **Cook the Eggs:**
    - In the same skillet, pour in the egg mixture. Cook, stirring gently, until the eggs are just set but still slightly soft. Remove from heat.
4. **Assemble the Quesadilla:**
    - Place one tortilla on a flat surface or plate. Sprinkle half of the shredded cheddar cheese evenly over the tortilla.
    - Spread the cooked spinach and any other vegetables over the cheese.
    - Spoon the scrambled eggs over the spinach and vegetables.
    - Sprinkle the remaining cheddar cheese on top and place the second tortilla over the filling, pressing down gently.
5. **Cook the Quesadilla:**
    - Wipe the skillet clean and return it to medium heat. Add a little more olive oil or butter if necessary.
    - Carefully transfer the assembled quesadilla to the skillet. Cook for about 2-3 minutes on each side, or until the tortilla is golden brown and crispy and the cheese is melted inside.
    - Press down gently with a spatula to ensure even cooking.
6. **Serve:**

- Remove the quesadilla from the skillet and let it cool for a minute before cutting it into wedges.
 - Serve with salsa, sour cream, or any additional toppings you like.

Tips:

- **Customizations:** Feel free to add other ingredients like cooked bacon, sausage, or tomatoes to make the quesadilla even heartier.
- **Cheese Options:** Besides cheddar, you can use other cheeses like Monterey Jack, feta, or mozzarella for different flavors.
- **Spice It Up:** Add a pinch of red pepper flakes or some chopped jalapeños if you like a bit of heat.

This Spinach and Cheddar Breakfast Quesadilla is versatile, satisfying, and easy to make, making it a great addition to your breakfast or brunch menu. Enjoy!

Green Apple and Cinnamon Breakfast Bars

Ingredients:

- 1 cup rolled oats
- 1/2 cup whole wheat flour
- 1/2 cup almond meal (or additional flour if preferred)
- 1/4 cup brown sugar or coconut sugar
- 1/2 tsp ground cinnamon
- 1/4 tsp ground nutmeg
- 1/4 tsp baking powder
- 1/4 tsp salt
- 1/2 cup unsweetened applesauce
- 1/4 cup honey or maple syrup
- 1 large egg
- 1 medium green apple, peeled, cored, and diced
- Optional: 1/4 cup chopped nuts or seeds (e.g., walnuts, almonds, chia seeds)

Instructions:

1. **Preheat Oven:**
   - Preheat your oven to 350°F (175°C).
   - Line an 8x8-inch baking pan with parchment paper or lightly grease it.
2. **Prepare Dry Ingredients:**
   - In a large bowl, combine the rolled oats, whole wheat flour, almond meal, brown sugar, ground cinnamon, ground nutmeg, baking powder, and salt. Mix well.
3. **Prepare Wet Ingredients:**
   - In a separate bowl, whisk together the applesauce, honey or maple syrup, and the egg until smooth and well combined.
4. **Combine Ingredients:**
   - Add the wet ingredients to the dry ingredients and stir until just combined.
   - Fold in the diced green apple and, if using, the chopped nuts or seeds.
5. **Bake:**
   - Spread the mixture evenly in the prepared baking pan.
   - Bake in the preheated oven for 25-30 minutes, or until the bars are golden brown and a toothpick inserted into the center comes out clean.
6. **Cool and Slice:**
   - Allow the bars to cool in the pan for about 10 minutes before transferring them to a wire rack to cool completely.
   - Once cooled, cut into squares or bars.

Tips:

- **Apples:** For extra flavor, you can toss the diced apples in a bit of cinnamon before adding them to the mixture.

- **Texture:** If you prefer a chunkier texture, you can coarsely chop the apples and mix them in. For a smoother texture, grate the apples.
- **Storage:** Store the bars in an airtight container at room temperature for up to a week, or refrigerate for longer shelf life.

These Green Apple and Cinnamon Breakfast Bars are a great way to enjoy a healthy and delicious breakfast or snack on the go. They're packed with fiber and natural sweetness, making them both nutritious and satisfying. Enjoy!

Irish Breakfast Tea Cake

Ingredients:

- 1 cup (240 ml) strong brewed Irish breakfast tea, cooled
- 1/2 cup (115 g) unsalted butter, room temperature
- 1 cup (200 g) granulated sugar
- 2 large eggs
- 2 cups (240 g) all-purpose flour
- 1 1/2 tsp baking powder
- 1/2 tsp baking soda
- 1/4 tsp salt
- 1/2 cup (120 ml) buttermilk (or milk with 1 tbsp lemon juice or vinegar)
- 1/2 cup (80 g) dried fruit (such as raisins, currants, or chopped dates) (optional)
- 1/2 tsp ground cinnamon (optional)
- 1/4 tsp ground nutmeg (optional)
- Powdered sugar for dusting (optional)

Instructions:

1. **Preheat Oven:**
    - Preheat your oven to 350°F (175°C).
    - Grease and flour an 8-inch round or square cake pan, or line it with parchment paper.
2. **Prepare Dry Ingredients:**
    - In a medium bowl, whisk together the flour, baking powder, baking soda, salt, cinnamon, and nutmeg (if using).
3. **Cream Butter and Sugar:**
    - In a large bowl, cream together the butter and granulated sugar until light and fluffy using an electric mixer, about 3-4 minutes.
4. **Add Eggs:**
    - Beat in the eggs, one at a time, until well combined.
5. **Combine Tea and Buttermilk:**
    - Stir in the cooled brewed tea and buttermilk until well combined.
6. **Mix Dry Ingredients:**
    - Gradually add the dry ingredients to the wet mixture, mixing until just combined. Do not overmix.
7. **Add Dried Fruit (Optional):**
    - Fold in the dried fruit if using.
8. **Pour Batter into Pan:**
    - Pour the batter into the prepared cake pan and spread it evenly.
9. **Bake:**
    - Bake in the preheated oven for 35-45 minutes, or until a toothpick inserted into the center of the cake comes out clean.
10. **Cool:**

- Allow the cake to cool in the pan for about 10 minutes, then transfer it to a wire rack to cool completely.
11. **Dust with Powdered Sugar (Optional):**
    - Once cooled, dust with powdered sugar if desired for a touch of sweetness.

Tips:

- **Tea Strength:** Use a strong brewed Irish breakfast tea for the best flavor. You can brew a bit more tea and use the excess in the recipe.
- **Add-ins:** You can also add chopped nuts or chocolate chips to the batter for extra texture and flavor.
- **Storage:** Store the tea cake in an airtight container at room temperature for up to a week, or freeze for longer storage.

This Irish Breakfast Tea Cake pairs beautifully with a cup of tea, making it a perfect choice for afternoon tea or a cozy breakfast treat. Enjoy!

Shamrock and Berry Smoothie

Ingredients:

- 1 cup fresh spinach leaves (for the "shamrock" green color)
- 1/2 cup frozen strawberries
- 1/2 cup frozen blueberries
- 1 banana, peeled and sliced
- 1/2 cup Greek yogurt (plain or vanilla)
- 1/2 cup almond milk (or any milk of your choice)
- 1 tbsp honey or maple syrup (optional, for added sweetness)
- 1/4 tsp vanilla extract (optional)
- Ice cubes (optional, for a thicker consistency)

Instructions:

1. **Prepare Ingredients:**
   - Place the fresh spinach leaves, frozen strawberries, frozen blueberries, and banana slices into a blender.
2. **Add Yogurt and Milk:**
   - Add the Greek yogurt and almond milk to the blender.
3. **Sweeten (Optional):**
   - If you like a sweeter smoothie, add honey or maple syrup. You can also add vanilla extract for extra flavor.
4. **Blend:**
   - Blend the ingredients on high speed until smooth and creamy. If the smoothie is too thick, you can add a bit more milk or water to reach your desired consistency.
5. **Adjust Consistency (Optional):**
   - For a thicker smoothie, add a few ice cubes and blend again until smooth.
6. **Serve:**
   - Pour the smoothie into glasses and serve immediately.

Tips:

- **Fresh vs. Frozen:** You can use fresh berries if you prefer, but frozen berries give the smoothie a thicker and colder texture.
- **Spinach Substitute:** If you prefer a different green, you can use kale or another leafy green in place of spinach.
- **Add-ins:** You can also add a spoonful of chia seeds, flax seeds, or protein powder for an extra nutritional boost.

This Shamrock and Berry Smoothie is not only visually appealing with its vibrant green color and red and blue berries but also packed with nutrients. It's a great way to start your day or to enjoy as a healthy snack!

Potato and Spinach Stuffed Croissants

Ingredients:

- 1 sheet of puff pastry or 1 can of refrigerated croissant dough (8-count)
- 1 medium potato, peeled and diced
- 1 cup fresh spinach leaves, chopped
- 1/2 cup shredded cheddar cheese (or cheese of your choice)
- 1 small onion, finely chopped
- 1 clove garlic, minced
- 1 tbsp olive oil
- Salt and black pepper to taste
- 1/4 tsp paprika (optional)
- 1/4 tsp dried thyme (optional)
- 1 egg, beaten (for egg wash)

Instructions:

1. **Prepare the Filling:**
    - Boil or steam the diced potato until tender, about 10 minutes. Drain and mash with a fork or potato masher. Set aside.
    - In a skillet, heat the olive oil over medium heat. Add the chopped onion and cook until softened and translucent, about 3-4 minutes.
    - Add the minced garlic and cook for another 1 minute until fragrant.
    - Stir in the chopped spinach and cook until wilted, about 2 minutes. Remove from heat.
    - Combine the mashed potato, spinach mixture, and shredded cheddar cheese in a bowl. Season with salt, black pepper, paprika, and dried thyme. Mix well.
2. **Prepare the Croissant Dough:**
    - If using puff pastry, roll it out slightly on a floured surface and cut it into squares (about 4x4 inches). If using croissant dough, separate the dough into triangles.
    - Place a spoonful of the potato and spinach filling in the center of each square or triangle of dough.
3. **Assemble the Croissants:**
    - For puff pastry, fold the corners of the dough over the filling to create a packet or fold the dough into a triangle shape, pinching the edges to seal.
    - For croissant dough, roll up each triangle from the wide end to the tip, pinching the sides to seal and form a crescent shape.
4. **Brush with Egg Wash:**
    - Place the stuffed croissants on a baking sheet lined with parchment paper.
    - Brush the tops of the croissants with the beaten egg to give them a golden brown finish.
5. **Bake:**
    - Bake in the preheated oven at 375°F (190°C) for 15-20 minutes, or until the croissants are golden brown and the filling is heated through.

6. **Cool and Serve:**
    - Allow the croissants to cool slightly before serving.

Tips:

- **Variations:** Feel free to add other ingredients to the filling, such as cooked bacon, sausage, or mushrooms, for additional flavor.
- **Spices and Herbs:** Adjust the seasoning to your taste. Fresh herbs like dill or parsley can be added for extra flavor.
- **Make Ahead:** You can prepare the filling ahead of time and store it in the refrigerator for up to 2 days. Assemble and bake the croissants when ready to serve.

These Potato and Spinach Stuffed Croissants are both satisfying and versatile, making them a perfect addition to any meal. Enjoy the flaky, buttery texture combined with the savory, flavorful filling!

Irish Breakfast Baked Oatmeal

Ingredients:

- 2 cups rolled oats
- 1/2 cup steel-cut oats (optional, for added texture)
- 1/4 cup brown sugar or maple syrup (adjust to taste)
- 1 tsp ground cinnamon
- 1/2 tsp ground nutmeg
- 1/2 tsp baking powder
- 1/4 tsp salt
- 1 1/2 cups milk (or any plant-based milk)
- 1/2 cup plain Greek yogurt (or any yogurt of your choice)
- 2 large eggs
- 1 tsp vanilla extract
- 1/2 cup raisins or currants
- 1/2 cup chopped nuts (such as walnuts or pecans) (optional)
- 1/2 cup chopped apples or pears (optional, for added fruitiness)
- 2 tbsp melted butter or coconut oil (for greasing the pan)

Instructions:

1. **Preheat Oven:**
   - Preheat your oven to 375°F (190°C).
   - Grease an 8x8-inch baking dish with melted butter or coconut oil.
2. **Combine Dry Ingredients:**
   - In a large bowl, mix together the rolled oats, steel-cut oats (if using), brown sugar, ground cinnamon, ground nutmeg, baking powder, and salt.
3. **Prepare Wet Ingredients:**
   - In another bowl, whisk together the milk, Greek yogurt, eggs, and vanilla extract until well combined.
4. **Mix Ingredients:**
   - Pour the wet ingredients into the dry ingredients and mix until everything is well combined.
   - Fold in the raisins or currants, chopped nuts, and chopped apples or pears (if using).
5. **Transfer to Baking Dish:**
   - Spread the oatmeal mixture evenly in the prepared baking dish.
6. **Bake:**
   - Bake in the preheated oven for 35-45 minutes, or until the top is golden brown and the oatmeal is set and firm in the center.
7. **Cool and Serve:**
   - Allow the baked oatmeal to cool slightly before cutting into squares or serving.
8. **Optional Toppings:**

- Serve warm with a drizzle of milk or yogurt, and a sprinkle of additional cinnamon or fresh fruit if desired.

Tips:

- **Make Ahead:** This baked oatmeal can be made ahead of time and stored in the refrigerator for up to 4 days. Reheat individual servings in the microwave or oven before serving.
- **Customization:** Feel free to customize the recipe with your favorite fruits, nuts, or spices. You can also add a handful of chocolate chips or coconut flakes for extra flavor.
- **Sweetness Level:** Adjust the sweetness to your preference by adding more or less brown sugar or maple syrup.

Irish Breakfast Baked Oatmeal is a nutritious and satisfying breakfast option that's perfect for busy mornings or leisurely weekends. Enjoy the hearty flavors and comforting warmth of this delicious dish!

Green Bell Pepper and Onion Frittata

Ingredients:

- 1 tbsp olive oil
- 1 medium green bell pepper, diced
- 1 small onion, finely chopped
- 6 large eggs
- 1/4 cup milk (or any milk of your choice)
- 1/2 cup shredded cheddar cheese (or cheese of your choice)
- 1/4 cup chopped fresh parsley or chives (optional, for garnish)
- Salt and black pepper to taste
- Optional: 1/2 cup cooked bacon or sausage, crumbled (for added protein)
- Optional: 1/4 tsp dried thyme or oregano (for extra flavor)

Instructions:

1. **Preheat Oven:**
   - Preheat your oven to 375°F (190°C). If using an oven-safe skillet, make sure it's preheated as well.
2. **Cook Vegetables:**
   - Heat the olive oil in an oven-safe skillet (such as a cast-iron skillet) over medium heat.
   - Add the diced green bell pepper and chopped onion to the skillet. Sauté for 5-7 minutes, or until the vegetables are tender and the onions are translucent.
3. **Prepare Egg Mixture:**
   - In a bowl, whisk together the eggs, milk, salt, black pepper, and dried herbs (if using). Mix until well combined.
4. **Combine Ingredients:**
   - If using cooked bacon or sausage, sprinkle it over the cooked vegetables.
   - Pour the egg mixture over the vegetables in the skillet. Stir gently to ensure the eggs are evenly distributed.
5. **Add Cheese:**
   - Sprinkle the shredded cheese evenly over the top of the egg mixture.
6. **Cook Frittata:**
   - Allow the frittata to cook on the stovetop for 2-3 minutes, until the edges start to set.
   - Transfer the skillet to the preheated oven and bake for 12-15 minutes, or until the frittata is fully set and lightly golden on top. A knife inserted into the center should come out clean.
7. **Cool and Serve:**
   - Allow the frittata to cool for a few minutes before slicing.
   - Garnish with fresh parsley or chives, if desired.
8. **Serve:**

- Serve warm or at room temperature. This frittata pairs well with a simple green salad or fresh fruit.

Tips:

- **Cheese Options:** Feel free to use any cheese you prefer, such as feta, goat cheese, or mozzarella.
- **Vegetable Variations:** You can add other vegetables like mushrooms, spinach, or tomatoes to the frittata for extra flavor and nutrition.
- **Storage:** Leftovers can be stored in the refrigerator for up to 4 days and can be enjoyed cold or reheated.

This Green Bell Pepper and Onion Frittata is a nutritious and satisfying dish that's easy to make and perfect for any meal of the day. Enjoy the vibrant flavors and the convenience of a one-pan meal!

Minted Yogurt and Berry Parfait

Ingredients:

- 2 cups plain Greek yogurt (or any yogurt of your choice)
- 2 tbsp honey or maple syrup (adjust to taste)
- 1 tsp vanilla extract
- 1 cup mixed fresh berries (such as strawberries, blueberries, raspberries, and blackberries)
- 2 tbsp fresh mint leaves, finely chopped
- 1/4 cup granola (optional, for added crunch)
- 1 tbsp chia seeds (optional, for extra nutrition)
- Fresh mint leaves for garnish (optional)

Instructions:

1. **Prepare Yogurt Mixture:**
    - In a bowl, mix the Greek yogurt with honey or maple syrup and vanilla extract. Stir until smooth and well combined.
2. **Prepare Mint:**
    - Finely chop the fresh mint leaves and fold them into the yogurt mixture. This will infuse the yogurt with a refreshing mint flavor.
3. **Layer the Parfait:**
    - In serving glasses or bowls, start by adding a layer of the minted yogurt.
    - Add a layer of mixed fresh berries on top of the yogurt.
    - If using, sprinkle a layer of granola and chia seeds over the berries.
4. **Repeat Layers:**
    - Repeat the layers with the remaining yogurt, berries, granola, and chia seeds.
5. **Garnish:**
    - Top the parfaits with additional fresh berries and a few mint leaves for garnish.
6. **Serve:**
    - Serve immediately, or cover and refrigerate for up to 2 hours to allow the flavors to meld.

Tips:

- **Berry Variations:** Use any combination of fresh berries you like. You can also use frozen berries, but be sure to thaw them and drain excess moisture before layering.
- **Sweetness:** Adjust the sweetness of the yogurt mixture to your taste. You can also use flavored yogurt if you prefer a different flavor profile.
- **Make-Ahead:** This parfait can be made ahead of time for a quick and easy breakfast or snack. Just be sure to add granola right before serving to keep it crunchy.

This Minted Yogurt and Berry Parfait is not only visually appealing but also packed with vitamins, minerals, and antioxidants. It's a delightful way to enjoy a healthy and satisfying meal or treat!

Irish Ham and Cheese Breakfast Roll-ups

Ingredients:

- 4 large flour tortillas
- 4 oz (115 g) Irish cheddar cheese, shredded (or cheese of your choice)
- 4 slices Irish ham (or any ham), sliced
- 2 large eggs
- 1/4 cup milk
- 1 tbsp butter or oil for cooking
- 2 tbsp chopped fresh chives or parsley (optional, for added flavor)
- Salt and black pepper to taste
- Optional: 1/4 tsp dried thyme or rosemary for additional flavor

Instructions:

1. **Prepare Egg Mixture:**
   - In a bowl, whisk together the eggs, milk, salt, and black pepper until well combined.
2. **Cook the Eggs:**
   - Heat a non-stick skillet over medium heat and add the butter or oil.
   - Pour the egg mixture into the skillet and cook, stirring occasionally, until the eggs are just set but still slightly soft. Remove from heat and set aside.
3. **Assemble the Roll-ups:**
   - Lay out the flour tortillas on a flat surface.
   - Evenly distribute the shredded cheddar cheese over each tortilla.
   - Place a slice of ham on top of the cheese.
   - Spoon a portion of the cooked eggs onto the tortilla over the ham and cheese.
   - Sprinkle with chopped chives or parsley, and any optional herbs if using.
4. **Roll Up the Tortillas:**
   - Carefully roll up each tortilla tightly, starting from one end and rolling to the other, to enclose the filling.
5. **Cook the Roll-ups (Optional):**
   - For a crispy exterior, you can heat a skillet over medium heat and toast the roll-ups, seam side down, until golden brown and crispy, about 2 minutes per side. This step adds a nice texture and helps seal the edges.
6. **Slice and Serve:**
   - Slice each roll-up into bite-sized pieces if desired.
   - Serve warm, or at room temperature.

Tips:

- **Customizations:** Feel free to add other ingredients such as sautéed mushrooms, bell peppers, or spinach to the filling for extra flavor and nutrition.

- **Cheese Options:** If you can't find Irish cheddar, any sharp cheddar or your favorite cheese will work.
- **Make-Ahead:** These roll-ups can be made ahead of time and stored in the refrigerator for up to 3 days. Reheat in a skillet or microwave before serving.

Irish Ham and Cheese Breakfast Roll-ups are a versatile and tasty breakfast option that can be enjoyed on the go or served as part of a larger brunch spread. Enjoy the combination of savory ham, melted cheese, and fluffy eggs wrapped in a soft tortilla!

Green Banana Pancakes

Ingredients:

- 2 ripe bananas
- 1 cup fresh spinach or kale (stems removed)
- 1 cup all-purpose flour
- 1 tbsp sugar (optional, adjust to taste)
- 2 tsp baking powder
- 1/2 tsp baking soda
- 1/4 tsp salt
- 1 large egg
- 1 cup milk (or any plant-based milk)
- 1/2 tsp vanilla extract
- 2 tbsp melted butter or oil (for the batter)
- Butter or oil for cooking

Instructions:

1. **Prepare the Greens:**
   - In a blender, combine the fresh spinach or kale with the ripe bananas. Blend until smooth and well combined. This will be your green base.
2. **Prepare Dry Ingredients:**
   - In a large bowl, whisk together the flour, sugar (if using), baking powder, baking soda, and salt.
3. **Combine Wet Ingredients:**
   - In another bowl, whisk together the egg, milk, and vanilla extract. Stir in the melted butter or oil.
4. **Mix Batter:**
   - Pour the green banana mixture into the wet ingredients and mix until well combined.
   - Add the wet mixture to the dry ingredients and stir until just combined. The batter will be slightly lumpy, which is okay.
5. **Cook Pancakes:**
   - Heat a non-stick skillet or griddle over medium heat and lightly grease with butter or oil.
   - Pour 1/4 cup of batter onto the skillet for each pancake. Cook until bubbles start to form on the surface and the edges look set, about 2-3 minutes.
   - Flip the pancake and cook for another 1-2 minutes on the other side, until golden brown and cooked through.
6. **Serve:**
   - Serve the green banana pancakes warm with your favorite toppings, such as fresh fruit, maple syrup, honey, or a dollop of yogurt.

Tips:

- **Greens:** You can use spinach for a milder taste or kale for a slightly more robust flavor. Make sure to blend the greens thoroughly to avoid chunks.
- **Sweetness:** Adjust the sweetness of the pancakes by adding more or less sugar to the batter. You can also use sweetened yogurt or fruit toppings to enhance sweetness.
- **Flour Options:** If you prefer a whole grain option, you can substitute whole wheat flour or oat flour for part of the all-purpose flour.

These Green Banana Pancakes are not only colorful and fun but also a great way to sneak some greens into your diet. Enjoy the nutritious twist on a classic breakfast favorite!

Shamrock and Herb Scrambled Eggs

Ingredients:

- 6 large eggs
- 1/4 cup milk (or any milk of your choice)
- 1/2 cup fresh spinach, finely chopped
- 2 tbsp fresh parsley, finely chopped
- 1 tbsp fresh chives, finely chopped
- 1 tbsp fresh basil or dill, finely chopped (optional)
- 1/4 cup shredded cheese (such as cheddar or feta) (optional)
- 1 tbsp butter or oil (for cooking)
- Salt and black pepper to taste

Instructions:

1. **Prepare Ingredients:**
   - Finely chop the fresh spinach and herbs. You want them to be small enough to incorporate well into the eggs.
2. **Whisk Eggs:**
   - In a bowl, whisk together the eggs, milk, salt, and black pepper until well combined and slightly frothy.
3. **Add Greens and Herbs:**
   - Gently fold the chopped spinach and herbs into the egg mixture. If using cheese, you can fold it in at this stage as well.
4. **Heat Pan:**
   - Heat a non-stick skillet over medium-low heat and add the butter or oil. Allow it to melt and coat the bottom of the pan.
5. **Cook Eggs:**
   - Pour the egg mixture into the skillet. Let it sit undisturbed for a few seconds until the edges start to set.
   - Gently stir with a spatula, pushing the eggs from the edges toward the center. Continue to cook, stirring occasionally, until the eggs are just set but still slightly creamy. Be careful not to overcook them.
6. **Serve:**
   - Remove from heat immediately to avoid further cooking. Serve the scrambled eggs warm, garnished with additional fresh herbs if desired.

Tips:

- **Texture:** For creamier eggs, use a bit more milk or cream. Stir gently and cook over low heat to achieve a soft texture.
- **Cheese:** Adding cheese can enhance the flavor and make the eggs extra creamy. Try using sharp cheddar or crumbled feta for a different taste.

- **Herb Variations:** Feel free to experiment with other herbs like thyme or tarragon based on your preference.

These Shamrock and Herb Scrambled Eggs are a colorful and nutritious way to enjoy a classic breakfast. They're perfect for adding a festive touch to your morning routine or serving as a special treat on St. Patrick's Day. Enjoy!